Baseball's Greatest Sluggers

Exciting, in-depth profiles
of the five greatest sluggers
in baseball history—Babe Ruth,
Jimmy Foxx, Ted Williams,
Willie Mays and Hank Aaron.

MAJOR LEAGUE
LIBRARY

Baseball's Greatest Sluggers

by Bill Libby

illustrated with photographs

Random House · New York

For The Rev. Richard Fraser,
my oldest friend.

Library of Congress Cataloging in Publication Data
Libby, Bill.   Baseball's greatest sluggers.
(Major league library, 19)
SUMMARY: Profiles of five home run heroes: Babe Ruth, Hank Aaron, Jimmy Foxx, Ted Williams, and Willie Mays.
1. Baseball—Biography—Juvenile literature.
2. Batting (Baseball)—Juvenile literature. [1. Baseball—Biography] I. Title.
GV865.A1L47   796.357'092'2   [920]   72-11715
ISBN 0-394-82538-1   ISBN 0-394-92538-6 (GLB)

PHOTOGRAPH CREDITS: The Bettmann Archive, 54, 96; Brown Brothers, 22; Culver Pictures, 18; Malcolm Emmons, 91, 120, 125; Fred Roe, 65, 144; United Press International, endpapers, 10, 15, 31, 35, 39, 42, 50, 57, 58, 61, 75, 79, 82, 86, 88, 111, 116, 130, 137, 139, 147; Wide World Photos, 2, 27, 47, 69, 102, 106, 109, 119.
Cover photo by Tony Triolo for SPORTS ILLUSTRATED © Time Inc.

Contents

Acknowledgments

The author wishes to thank Bob Hope of the Atlanta Braves; Garry Schumacher of the San Francisco Giants; Harold Weissman of the New York Mets; Bob Broeg of the St. Louis *Post-Dispatch* and *The Sporting News*; Joe Cronin, president of the American League; and all the players, publicists, writers and executives who have contributed in various ways to this book.

Introduction

The slugger is the most glamorous player in baseball. Since 1920, when Babe Ruth first electrified the baseball world with his dramatic home runs, the power hitter has been the real star of the game.

Choosing the all-time best sluggers has been a challenge, and not everyone will agree with our selections. Since baseball is a game of statistics, we turned to the record book for the final decision. We studied five categories that seemed to encompass what baseball slugging is all about: home runs, extra-base hits, total bases, runs· batted in and slugging percentage. Each of the five sluggers in this book stood very near the top in all five categories. They are Babe Ruth, Jimmy Foxx, Ted Williams, Willie Mays and Hank Aaron.

The greatness of these five can hardly be doubted. They seem even greater when you consider the great hitters they surpassed—men like Lou Gehrig, Mel Ott, Stan Musial, Joe DiMaggio, Mickey Mantle and Frank Robinson. Some of these players did not play long enough to achieve top career records. Others fell far short in one or more of the five categories. They too had dramatic stories, and we wish we could have included them all.

Here, then, are the stories of the five greatest. They had very different personalities and different strengths and weaknesses. But they had one thing in common—few men in history could match their skill at hitting a baseball.

Baseball's Greatest Sluggers

⚾ *Babe Ruth*

He was born in 1895, began to play professional baseball in 1914, retired in 1935 and died in 1948. Yet he is as great a name in baseball today as he was at his peak. In the United States and other baseball-playing countries, the name "Babe Ruth" means baseball. Fans who never saw him play and who weren't born until after he died know his name as well as they know the names of today's stars.

Babe Ruth was so famous that he became a folk hero. As the stories about him were told over and over, he became a figure larger than life, a hero in a legend. In fact, it sometimes seems as though some story-teller made him up—like Tarzan or Superman. Yet he really did exist. He was a man like other men, with weaknesses as well as strengths. He was often heroic, but he was sometimes funny and sometimes sad. In a few short years he changed the shape of baseball and became a hero to millions. But he had enemies as well as friends, and his last years were marred by disappointments and sickness.

The year before Babe Ruth arrived in the majors, Frank "Home Run" Baker led the American League in home runs with eight. Baseball was a scientific, defensive game. The balls used were "dead" and scoring was scarce. Hitters choked up on light-weight bats, hit singles, stole bases and hustled for rare, precious runs.

Five years later, in 1918, Ruth led the league in homers for the first time with eleven. The next year he hit 29 and the next year 54—more than any other *team* in the league. The baseball world was amazed. This young player, who started out as a pitcher, had suddenly given the game muscle and explosive excitement. Baseball would never be quite the same again.

Ruth's personality and his strength at the plate brought thousands of new fans to the game. Baseball's team owners soon made it easier to hit home runs by developing a "live" ball that could be hit further and by bringing the outfield fences in toward the plate. The Babe profited by these developments, yet no one ever doubted that he was the most talented slugger who ever played the game. Thirty-five years after he retired, no one had matched his record of 60 home runs in a 154-game season or his lifetime total of 714.

But what kind of person was he? To begin with, he was a big man for his day, standing 6-foot-2 and weighing anywhere from 200 to 260 pounds. His enormous appetite for food and drink soon became famous. It was not unusual for him to have steak and whiskey for breakfast and a half-dozen lobsters and beer for a midnight snack. In between he would stuff himself with hot dogs, peanuts and soda pop.

It's no wonder that he often had stomach trouble. One of his favorite dishes was the pickled eels prepared by teammate Lou Gehrig's mother. Sometimes between games of a doubleheader Ruth would consume a jar of the eels mixed with a quart of chocolate ice cream.

Between seasons the Babe's weight would rise as high as 260 pounds. In the spring he sat in steam baths and dieted to the point of starvation to get down to playing weight. And every year his playing weight increased. His personal trainer once estimated that Ruth dieted off 1,000 pounds in his career.

Ruth was one of the rare athletes who could eat and drink to excess, keep irregular hours, and then perform brilliantly at the ballpark. Throughout his career he was fined and scolded for breaking training rules, yet to everyone's surprise, he could usually come through when it counted in a game.

Ruth hardly looked the part of a great athlete. His belly, which grew bigger as he got older, was supported on thin legs and pigeon-toed feet. He ran with short, mincing steps, almost lady-like. His face was round and wide with a wide nose, thick lips, laughing eyes and a ready grin. That homely face soon became one of the most familiar in America.

In his prime as the greatest player on one of the greatest teams in history, Ruth lived an independent life from the rest of his teammates. When they stayed in a fair hotel, he stayed in the best hotel in town, often paying $100 a day for his suite. Teams traveled mostly by train in those days, but on shorter trips players went by bus or were allowed to drive their own cars. The Babe bought an expensive, high-powered convertible for such trips and often chauffeured his friends along the narrow two-lane highways at fantastic speeds, singing all the way.

One night, returning from a game in Philadelphia, he ran his car off the road and wrecked it. Rumors spread that the Babe had been killed, and thousands of fans flocked to newspaper offices to find out if the rumor was true. Ruth, who was not even injured, came to the ballpark the next day and hit a home run.

"I'm not dead yet," he roared.

When the police stopped the Babe for speeding or reckless driving, they often let him go because they were his fans, too. Once in New York, some officers put him in jail rather than let him go with a summons, just so they could say they had spent some time with Babe Ruth.

Although Ruth was often rough and surly, he also had a child-like charm. One afternoon President Calvin Coolidge came to see him play. Introduced to the President, the Babe said, "Jeez, it's hot, ain't it, Prez?" The normally expressionless Coolidge, who was nicknamed "The Great Stone Face," broke into a broad grin.

The Babe was terrible with names. He seldom remembered even the names of his own teammates, and anyone he talked to he called "Kid" or "Pal" or "Doc." Yet he was amazingly responsive to his fans. Wherever he went he was recognized and mobbed. He seemed not to mind this attention and would spend hours after games signing autographs.

"I'd never turn down a kid," he once said. "They're the reason for the game which has been so good to me."

The Babe shows his classic swing.

His visits to sick children in hospitals became legendary even though he tried to keep many of his trips out of the newspapers. He always seemed genuinely moved by those who were sick or handicapped, and he often promised to hit home runs for them.

Beyond his behavior off the field was his baseball performance. He began as a pitcher and set several records before he was moved to the outfield. He was a good fielder with a strong arm, and he was even a pretty fair base runner. But it was hitting that made the Babe a hero.

How he could hit! He showed baseball a swing like it had never seen before, exploding into action as the ball approached, pivoting on his heels and twisting his body like a pretzel. His home run records are known to everyone: 60 home runs in a season, 714 in his career. But the rest of his batting accomplishments are often forgotten. One year he batted .393, and his lifetime average was .342, better than any player since his day except Ted Williams. In 1920 his slugging average was .847, and no player since 1935 has come within 100 points of that average. His lifetime slugging average was .693 and no player before or since has come within 60 points of it.

One or another of his records may be broken in future years, but few will ever match the Babe as an all-round hitter. He hit for average and for power, setting some records that seem almost impossible to match.

George Herman Ruth, Jr., was born February 6, 1895, at the home of his grandfather in a poor section of Baltimore. George Ruth, Sr., and his wife

Kate had eight children in all, but only two of them lived to maturity—George, Jr., who was the oldest, and Mayme.

The Babe's father had worked as a salesman, horse-cart driver and bartender. When George, Jr., was growing up, his father and his uncle were operating a saloon at 38 South Eutaw in a poor neighborhood of Baltimore. The Ruth family lived in rooms behind the saloon and young George soon learned to sweep up the bar, drink leftover beer and whiskey from the glasses on the tables and use the swear words he learned from the customers. Kate Ruth was often sick and unable to care for her children, so George was on his own from an early age.

He once told an interviewer, "I was chewing tobacco by the time I was seven. I was drinking hard whiskey by the time I was ten. I could cuss with anyone before I could spell my name. I was stealing in the streets and might have come to no good end if I hadn't been sent away young."

In June of 1902, when George was seven, there was a shooting in his father's saloon. The authorities who investigated the shooting urged the Ruth family to send George to St. Mary's Industrial School for Boys where he would be looked after more carefully. St. Mary's was a Roman Catholic protectory, part orphanage and part reformatory. From then on, George lived more at St. Mary's than at home. He seldom spoke of his parents in later years.

From the beginning he was rebellious and tough, resisting religious instruction and ignoring his school work. But he soon began to pay attention to athletics. During the baseball season the 800 boys at St. Mary's were divided by age and ability into 40 or more baseball teams which played regular schedule. against other teams of similar ability. Ruth had so much talent and learned baseball skills so quickly that he was soon advanced into competition with older players.

He also met Brother Matthias, a huge man who was responsible for punishing boys who broke the rules. Brother Matthias saw through Ruth's tough-

George Ruth, age 17, in a group photo at St. Mary's.

ness and eventually became almost a father to him.

"I had no one else, so I adopted him," the Babe admitted years later.

With Brother Matthias's encouragement, George began to take baseball seriously. Years later, when he was a young pitcher for the Boston Red Sox, he told *Baseball Magazine*, "When I was a kid, I used to play baseball most of the time. There was no 154-game schedule for us. The year we didn't get in more than 200 games was a slack season for us. I used to hit .450 or .500. I kept track one season and found that I made over 60 home runs. The last two years I pitched and got along pretty well. But I never lost my taste for hitting and don't ever expect to."

The coach of a rival school team, Brother Gilbert of Mt. St. Joseph's, was the man who brought Ruth to the attention of professional baseball. He called Jack Dunn, owner of the Baltimore Orioles, a team in the International League. Dunn went to see Ruth pitch and was enormously impressed. He offered the youngster $600 for his first season. The Babe was only 19 years old, not old enough to sign a contract. Jack Dunn became his legal guardian, Ruth signed the agreement with Dunn's approval, and St. Mary's gave him his release.

So in February 1914 Ruth went by bus to Fayetteville, North Carolina, to the Orioles' spring training camp. He was a green youngster with much to learn. The hotel in Fayetteville had an elevator and Ruth had never seen one before. At first he took it up and down and up and down just for the ride. He also discovered that he didn't have to pay for his meals, so he began ordering enormous quantities of food—not because he was so hungry, but because the food was free.

The other Orioles, many of them seasoned veterans, were amused by Ruth's innocence and enjoyed teasing him. Then one day coach Sam Steinman warned them, "You be careful with the teasing after Dunn gets down here. This boy is one of his babes."

The players began to call him "Babe" and the name stuck, soon to become the most famous name in baseball.

Jack Dunn was a shrewd baseball man and he turned down several offers for Ruth, knowing that the young player's value would increase. But as the 1914 season progressed, Dunn ran into financial trouble. Another professional team had come into Baltimore and was stealing his paying customers away. So he began to look for a buyer for Ruth. He finally offered a deal to Joe Lannin who owned the Boston Red Sox and Lannin bought Ruth for $2,900. It was one of the great buys in baseball history.

Ruth reported to Boston on July 11 and was scheduled to pitch against Cleveland the day he arrived. He pitched seven innings and got credit for a 4-3 victory. In his second start he lasted only four innings and was charged with the loss. The Red Sox decided he needed more minor league experience, so he was sent to their Providence team in the International League, where he played against his old Baltimore teammates.

He finished the season with a minor league record of 22 wins and 9 losses. Then he returned to the majors for the last few weeks of their longer season and won an 11-5 victory over the Yankees, bringing his major league record to 2-1.

Ruth started the 1915 season with Boston, but had a hard time, losing four of his first five decisions. But on May 6 he hit his first home run, against the New York Yankees. The next morning the New York *Times* reported, "For Boston, the big left-handed pitcher Babe Ruth was all that a pitcher was supposed to be and more. He put his team into the running with a home run rap into the upper tier in right field. First up in the third, with no apparent effort, he slammed a homer into the stands. . . ."

After his early losses, the Babe hit his pitching stride and won six in a row. He finished the season with an 18-8 record, helping the Red Sox win the pennant. He also hit .315 and chalked up four home runs. Bobby Roth led the league in homers that year with seven. The Red Sox won the World Series from the Philadelphia Phillies in five games before Ruth could make his scheduled start in the sixth game. He pinch-hit once, against Grover Cleveland Alexander, and struck out.

The next season Ruth became the best left-handed pitcher in the league. He won 23 and lost only 12, pitched nine shutouts and led the league with a 1.75 earned run average. The Red Sox won the pennant again and in the World Series the Babe started the second game against the Brooklyn Dodgers. In the first inning he gave up an inside-the-park home run when two of his outfielders collided. But then he blanked Brooklyn for 13 innings and the Red Sox won in the bottom of the 14th.

He continued his winning ways in 1917, winning 24 and losing 13. But the Red Sox finished second in the pennant race and the team was sold to a theatrical promoter named Harry Frazee. There was no

Ruth might have become baseball's greatest pitcher, but he was more valuable as a hitter.

way to know it at the time, but the change of owner-ship was important to Ruth's career.

In 1918 the Red Sox had a new manager named Ed Barrow, who had been brought in by Frazee. Early in the season, Barrow and his field captain Harry Hooper decided to play Ruth in the outfield when he wasn't pitching. So the Babe did a little of everything that year. He pitched in 20 games, win-ning 13 and losing 7. He filled in for a short time at first base and played 59 games in the outfield. Even with his limited playing time, he led the league in home runs for the first time with eleven.

The Red Sox won the pennant for the third time in Ruth's stay with the team, and they faced the Chicago Cubs in the World Series. Ruth pitched the opener and shut out the Cubs 1-0 on six hits. He pitched the fourth game and stopped Chicago 3-2 on seven hits. In this game he was not scored on until one was out in the eighth inning. Counting his 13 innings against Brooklyn in 1916 and nine innings in the first game against the Cubs, he had pitched 29⅔ scoreless innings in a row in Series competition. This stood as a record until 1961 when Whitey Ford of the Yankees broke it. The Red Sox won the Series in six games.

By 1919 the owner and the manager of the Red Sox realized that fans would come out to see a man like Ruth hit home runs. They determined to play him as much as possible even if his pitching suffered. Ruth responded by hitting a homer on opening day. By mid-season he had so many that historians were checking the records to see who had the most home runs in one season. They discovered that Ned Williamson was credited with 27 homers in 1884.

Late in September the Babe was approaching Williamson's record. On Babe Ruth day in Fenway Park, Boston, he clouted a line drive into the left-field seats—his 27th of the year. The next day he hit two more to finish the season with 29. He also hit .322 and drove in 114 runs. Unfortunately, the rest of the Red Sox did not have a good year, slipping from first to sixth place. And the owner, Harry Frazee, had had an even worse year, losing money on his theatrical productions. He desperately needed money and, like Jack Dunn years earlier, he decided to sell Babe Ruth.

"It was such a shame to let him go," outfielder Harry Hooper sighed years later. "Between 1912 and 1918 we won four pennants and four World Series. We had a bad year in 1918, but the Babe had a great year. He was really just beginning to roll, and with him we might have had the greatest dynasty of all time. But Harry Frazee was money-mad and soon sold most of our best players and ruined the team."

Frazee went to Colonel Jacob Ruppert, co-owner of the Yankees, and asked for the money he needed. Ruppert was eager to find a top star for the Yanks, since they had been second-best to the New York Giants for years. Ruppert offered $125,000 for Ruth and offered to arrange for an additional loan of $350,000. Frazee agreed, and Babe Ruth became a Yankee. The Boston fans were upset and angry, but New Yorkers were delighted when the sale was announced.

The Red Sox had bought the Babe for $2,900 in 1914. They had never paid him more than $10,000 a year and they sold him six seasons later for $125,000. The Babe was already the most valuable player in baseball, but he was only beginning his amazing career.

In 1920 the Yankees paid him $20,000 (which was worth nearly $100,000 in today's currency), and he rewarded his team handsomely. He hit .356 and slugged 54 home runs, more than any other *team* in the American League. His slugging average was .847. No other player has ever approached this one-season average. The Yankees, who had been playing in the New York Giants' Polo Grounds for years, soon made plans for a new stadium. Although it was to be called Yankee Stadium, it became known at the time as "the House that Ruth Built"—with good reason. In 1920 in the Polo Grounds, the revitalized Yanks drew nearly 1,300,000 fans and they finished in third place, only three games out of the lead.

The next year the Babe hit 59 homers, drove in 170 runs (setting a major league record) and batted .378. His slugging average of .846 was down only one point from the previous year. Baseball had never seen hitting like this. The Yanks finished first in the American League for the first time in their 20-year history. In the World Series they faced their home-town rivals, the New York Giants, and all games were played in the Polo Grounds. Ruth hit his first Series home run in the fourth game but then was sidelined with an injury for the last games of the Series, and the Giants won, five games to three. This was the last World Series in which the winner had to take five games.

The Babe was beginning to see what he was worth to baseball. For the 1922 season he asked and got $52,000, an astonishing figure for those days. When a sportswriter wondered why Ruth wanted exactly $52,000, the Babe replied with a grin, "I always wanted to make a thousand bucks a week."

But before the season began, Ruth took some of his lesser-known teammates on a long barnstorming tour of the United States even though he knew it was against baseball rules. The stern baseball commissioner, Kenesaw Mountain Landis, promptly suspended the barnstormers for the first month of the 1922 season.

Ruth didn't get into action until late May and didn't really get going all year. He played in 110 games and hit only .315 with 35 homers. The Yanks managed to win the pennant, but they lost the World Series to the Giants again, this time in four straight games. It was a bad year for the Babe, although most other ballplayers would have been happy to do so well.

In 1923 the Yanks finally had their own park, thanks to Babe Ruth. On the first game in the new Yankee Stadium, the Babe rose to the occasion by hitting a three-run homer to beat the Red Sox 4-1. He had a spectacular year, batting .393 with 130 RBI's and 41 homers. In addition, he set a major league record by walking 170 times. By now the pitchers were afraid of him and would rather allow him one base than risk giving him four.

The Yanks won the pennant and for the third year in a row they faced the New York Giants in the World Series. The first World Series home run in Yankee Stadium was hit by the Giant center fielder, Casey Stengel, who would one day rank with Ruth as a Yankee hero after managing the Yanks to ten pennants in twelve years. But the Babe hit three homers himself and batted .386 as the Yanks won their first world championship.

The Babe had another good year in 1924, winning his first batting championship with a .378 average. But in 1925 he reported to spring training heavier than ever. When the team began to travel north, the Babe played host to 1,000 orphans at an exhibition game in Nashville. That afternoon he put on one of his amazing eating displays, downing endless numbers of hot dogs and soda. That night as the Yankee

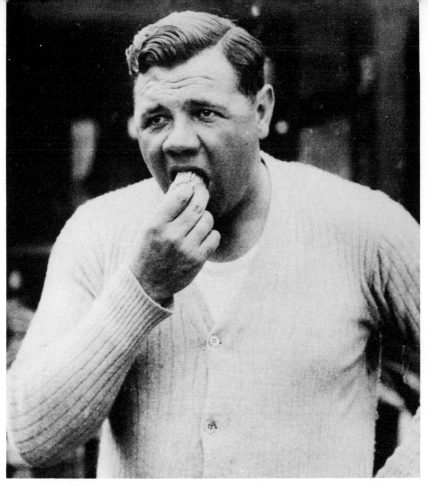

The Babe was almost as great an eater as he was a hitter.

train headed north again, he was stricken with terrific stomach pains. He was rushed to the hospital and some newspapers reported that he was near death. He did require surgery, and the whole country followed the medical bulletins until the great hero was out of danger. He didn't get into the Yankee line-up until June 1 and he was still out of shape.

As the Yankees fell into a dismal slump, the Babe continued his high jinks off the field. Late in August he broke curfew in St. Louis. When scolded by pep-

pery manager Miller Huggins the next day, the Babe
shrugged and said that he had had "personal business" to attend to. Huggins, whose team had slipped
deep into the second division, had lost patience with
Ruth. He suspended him and fined him $5,000.

Ruth was furious. "If you were bigger, I'd punch
you in the nose," he reportedly told Huggins.

Huggins replied, "You're not as big a man as you
think you are."

Ruth told the press that he would leave the
Yankees if Huggins stayed as manager. The Babe
seemed sure that the Yankee owner would side with
him against the manager. But after a private meeting
with Huggins, a subdued Ruth apologized publicly
for his rash remarks. Still, Huggins kept him out of
the line-up for almost a month.

The season ended dismally for both Ruth and the
Yanks. The Babe hit only 25 homers and his average
fell below .300 for the first time since he quit pitching. After a dozen years in the majors it looked as if
his undisciplined life was ruining his baseball career.

There was one bright spot in the year for the Yankees, however. On June 1, the same day that Ruth
returned to the line-up, a youngster named Lou
Gehrig had come up as a pinch hitter. The next day
he filled in for first baseman Wally Pipp. Pipp never
got back into the regular line-up, and for the next
ten years Gehrig provided a bat for the Yankees that
almost equaled Ruth's.

Like Ruth, Henry Louis Gehrig, Jr., was the son of
German immigrants. But in almost all other ways he
was different. He was as quiet and reserved as the
Babe was loud and brash. A powerful 6-foot-1, 212-
pounder, he had wide hips, a prominent rear end

and heavy legs. He had attended Columbia University and he gave the impression of being shy and studious. But on the field, he was soon challenging the Babe himself. In 1926 Gehrig hit .313.

Ruth, who had announced to the world that he had "reformed," did as he had promised—he made good all over again, batting .372, driving in 155 runs and slamming 47 homers. The Yanks moved back up to first place, but lost the World Series to the St. Louis Cardinals in seven hard-fought games.

In 1927 the Yankees fielded what many people consider the greatest team in history. Standing high above the others were Ruth and Gehrig. The Babe hit .356, drove in 164 runs and hit his famous 60 homers. But Gehrig outdid Ruth, hitting .378, driving in a record-shattering 175 runs and hitting 47 homers. He was later voted Most Valuable Player in the American League. The Yanks won 110 games and finished 19 games ahead of the League.

By season's end, however, all eyes were on the Babe and his home run pace. Going into September he had hit only 43. Then he exploded. In the next-to-last game of the season, with the Yanks behind, the Babe came up and walloped his 60th of the season into the right-field stands.

The New York *Times* reported the next day, "Hats were tossed in the air, papers were torn up and thrown liberally, and the spirit of celebration permeated the place. The Babe's stroll to his outfield position [after the inning] was the signal for a handkerchief salute in which all the bleacherites to the last man participated. Jovial Babe entered into the carnival spirit and punctuated his strides with a succession of snappy military salutes."

In the World Series, the world-beating Yanks were facing the Pittsburgh Pirates. After watching the awesome Yank line-up, called "Murderers' Row," in batting practice, the Pirates seemed shaken. They promptly lost four straight games as the Babe hit two home runs, averaged .400 and drove in seven runs.

The sportswriters tried to outdo each other in finding new nicknames for the Babe. He was called the "Sultan of Swat," the "King of Clout," and "Bambino" (Italian for "Babe"). Everywhere he went, crowds came out, hoping to see him hit another homer.

He used the heaviest bat he could find. It was a dark piece of lumber which he nicknamed "Black Betsy." It weighed 52 ounces. Many players today use bats that weigh as little as 32 ounces. The Babe said, "My theory is, the bigger the bat, the faster the ball will travel."

He stood well back in the batter's box and a few inches behind the plate. He stepped into the ball and the power of his swing would often bring him to one knee. Most of his home runs were pulled to right field, but he was perfectly able to hit to the opposite field as well. He had amazing eyesight, lightning reflexes and tremendous strength. If the ball did not go out of the park, it was usually tough for the fielders to handle.

The Yanks won the pennant again in 1928 behind Ruth's 54 homers. Ruth and Gehrig each drove in 142 runs. In the World Series they took apart the St. Louis Cardinals, winning four straight games as Ruth hit .625 and Gehrig hit .545.

In the last game of the Series, Cardinal pitcher

Bill Sherdel threw a third strike past the Babe before he was set. The Babe protested that it was an illegal "quick pitch," and the umpire agreed that it should be thrown over.

"I'll hit it for a homer just to show the wise guy," Ruth told the umpire.

He did just that, slamming one of his three home runs in the game.

Of all his great talents, the most amazing was this ability to call his shots. On another occasion he hit a ball into the stands, but the umpire ruled it "foul by an inch."

Ruth was angry and boasted to the umpire that he would hit the next one an inch fair. He hit a towering drive down the foul line into the stands and

Ruth hits one of his three homers in the fourth game of the 1926 World Series.

stood at the plate awaiting the umpire's decision.

"Go on," growled the umpire. "It's an inch fair."

In 1929 the Babe had another banner year, but the Yankees lost the pennant to the Philadelphia Athletics. The A's boasted a new young slugger named Jimmy Foxx. Late in the season, Yankee Manager Miller Huggins fell ill of blood poisoning. On September 25 he died. Ruth, who had had many bitter fights with the little manager, was in tears. "A great little guy has left us," he said. "He was never looking for any glory or bragging about himself. We had a few battles, but there was no man that I liked better in baseball."

Looking forward to the 1930 season, the Babe was hoping that he would be made the new manager. Many observers laughed at the idea. As someone said, he couldn't manage himself, much less a whole team. Bob Shawkey was named the new manager and Ruth was given a new contract calling for $80,000 a year. When someone pointed out that this was more than President Hoover made, Babe replied, "I had a better year than he did."

The Babe had two more good seasons, hitting 49 and 46 home runs and batting .359 and .373. But by the end of the 1931 season, his legs were starting to weaken and Yankee fans sometimes taunted him. His baserunning was poor and his fielding suffered. In August of 1931 he hit his 600th homer. Although his performance was still spectacular, the Babe was beginning to decline. The Yanks finished far behind Philadelphia both years.

In 1932 a new home run king was crowned. Jimmy Foxx of Philadelphia set out after the Babe's record of 60 in one year and fell only two short, finishing the season with 58. Ruth hit 41 and it was the first year since 1925 that he failed to lead the league.

While Foxx was passing Ruth, the Yankees were coming back to pass Philadelphia. They won the pennant by 13 games and faced the Chicago Cubs in the World Series. Ruth's legs were sore and the long season had tired him, but he could still hit, as the Cubs were to find out in one of the highlights of his career.

As the Series started, the Yankees were taunting the Cubs. To make things worse, the Yanks won the first two games by scores of 12-6 and 5-2. When the third game opened in Chicago, Cub fans rallied to their team's support. When Ruth came up in the first inning, they booed him. He hit a three-run homer. Returning to his position in the field, he tipped his cap to the fans, making them angrier than ever.

Then the Babe made a bad play in the outfield and the fans showered him with garbage. A lemon hit him in the leg. He pointed to his legs and shook his head, seeming to say, "Don't hit me there." Then he pointed to his head and nodded, as if to say, "If you have to hit me, hit me in the head where I won't feel it."

The Babe narrowly missed a home run in the third inning and the crowd taunted him louder than ever. When he came up in the fifth, the Cub players in the dugout began to razz him too. Now all the insults seemed to be getting to him. "They called me 'baboon' and 'big-belly,' " he recalled later.

Ruth was facing Cub pitcher Charlie Root. Before the first pitch the Babe held up three fingers as if to tell Root that he needed three strikes. The first pitch was a strike. The Babe held up two fingers—"two strikes left." Finally, with the count two balls and two strikes, Ruth held up one finger and pointed to the center field wall. Root pitched and the Babe drove the ball over the wall exactly where he had pointed.

Whether or not the Babe really called his shot has been debated ever since, but the Babe himself always insisted he had. He called it "the proudest moment of my career," and said, "I just laughed all the way around the bases, saying to myself, 'You lucky bum!' " The Yankees won the game and disposed of the Cubs in four straight to sweep the Series again.

Ruth's career was now coming to an end. Before the 1933 season he turned 38. The Great Depression had made fans and money scarce in baseball, and the Babe took a big salary cut. He still batted .301 and hit 34 homers, but it was a struggle. Some of the other Yankee stars had faded, too, and the world champs finished the season in second place.

In 1934 the Babe huffed and puffed and limped to a .288 average and only 22 homers. He hit his 700th on July 13th and finished the season with 708, but time was running out. Although Lou Gehrig won the Triple Crown and was named Most Valuable Player for the third time, the Yanks finished in second place again.

After the final game of the season, Ruth went to Yankee owner Jake Ruppert and asked once more for the job as manager. Ruppert refused and Ruth said, "All right, I am leaving the Yankees and retiring from baseball." He left for an exhibition tour of Japan as the news of his retirement swept the country.

Baseball's greatest one-two punch, Gehrig and Ruth, as they appeared in 1935.

When he returned from Japan, Ruth took back his retirement announcement and accepted an offer from the Boston Braves to be a player-coach. In the Braves' opening game of 1935, the 40-year-old wonder singled home one run, scored another and then won the game with a two-run homer. But as the season progressed, it was clear that the Babe was through. His batting average hovered around .200 and his fielding and base-running were terrible.

He had one more magic moment. On May 25th

the Braves played the Pittsburgh Pirates, and several of the Pirates began to taunt the fat old man in batting practice. Ruth replied by hitting three home runs, the last one a towering drive off the roof of the three-tiered stands.

He appeared in a few more games, but that mighty clout in Pittsburgh turned out to be the last home run he would hit in the major leagues. He was arguing with the Braves' management and performing poorly on the field. Finally, he called the writers together and said, "I'm sorry to have to tell you this, boys, but this is it."

In the following years the Babe drifted in and out of the fringes of baseball, making special guest appearances and signing autographs for a new generation of fans. In 1938 he was a coach for the Brooklyn Dodgers for half the season, but that was his last official connection with a major league team.

Meanwhile, the Yankees were prospering again. They won the pennant in 1937 and 1938 led by Lou Gehrig and a new outfielder, Joe DiMaggio. Then in 1939 Gehrig suddenly slumped. Within a few weeks he was out of the line-up and it soon became known that he was suffering from a fatal disease. On the Fourth of July, the Babe returned to Yankee Stadium for Lou Gehrig Day. The two sluggers had not always gotten along, but on this day they met on the field, hugged each other and wept unashamedly. Less than two years later Lou Gehrig died.

A few years later the Babe himself was stricken with an incurable disease—cancer of the throat. On June 13, 1948, he returned once more to Yankee Stadium to celebrate the 25th anniversary of the Yanks' first World Championship. He had to be helped into his old uniform, which now hung loosely on his wasted frame. He spoke to the crowd over a microphone in a hoarse whisper. "You know how bad my voice sounds," he said. "Well, it feels just as bad."

Two months later Ruth died.

More than 100,000 people filed past his casket, which lay in state at Yankee Stadium. The day of his funeral was hot and muggy. After the service the pallbearers were standing outside the church in the hot sun. Old third baseman Joe Dugan whispered to Waite Hoyt, "I'd give almost anything for a cold beer."

"So would the Babe," Hoyt replied.

He had been one of the first players elected to the Hall of Fame in 1936, and when he died he still held the most amazing set of baseball records ever held by one man: first in home runs (714), runs batted in (2,217), slugging average (.690), and extra base hits (1,356).

But his place in baseball depended on more than records. Waite Hoyt, a top pitcher for the Yankees during Ruth's heyday, was once asked if there would ever be another Ruth.

"Don't be silly," he said. "Oh sure, somebody came along who hit more than 60 home runs in a season and somebody may come who can hit more than 714, but that wouldn't make either of them another Ruth.

"His appeal was to the emotions. He was the greatest crowd-pleaser of them all. He made moments in baseball that will remain magical forever. Another Ruth? Never!"

⚾ Jimmy Foxx

Before Babe Ruth retired, another great slugger had come onto the scene. He was a heavily-muscled young man named Jimmy Foxx, and during the 1932 season he would even threaten the Babe's single-season home run record of 60. Foxx would also beat Ruth out of two Most Valuable Player awards and come to be known as "The Right-Handed Ruth."

Yet Jimmy Foxx never attracted the attention or the salary of Babe Ruth. He was an amazing hitter, but he was no showman on or off the field. He was a gentle, quiet man, very unlike the colorful Ruth, who overshadowed him from the start.

When others complained that Jimmy didn't receive his fair share of attention, he would smile and say, "It's all right, it's a lot of fun anyway." But it's sad, really, because of all the super-sluggers in baseball, Jimmy Foxx is still the least known and remembered. There have been no books written about him, and many fans who still marvel at Ruth have never even heard of "Old Double-X."

Like Ruth, Foxx was from Maryland and was often called "The Maryland Strong-Man." He was also sometimes called "The Beast." He stood just under six feet tall and weighed over 200 pounds. He had big biceps and huge forearms and hands that made his bat seem like a twig.

Foxx had a ferocious swing and struck out over 1,300 times in his career, but he hit for consistency as well as power. He hit .340 or better in six seasons, with highs of .364 and .360, and he won the batting championship twice. One year he won the Triple Crown (batting average, homers and RBI's) and narrowly missed it on two other occasions. He drove in 100 or more runs in 13 straight seasons and hit 30 or

more home runs in twelve seasons in a row.

Some of Jimmy's homers became legends. He hit the longest drive ever recorded out of Chicago's Comiskey Park. The ball cleared the double-decked stands and landed in a playground outside the ballpark, traveling an estimated 600 feet. He hit another drive just as long in Philadelphia's old Shibe Park, and he almost became the only man ever to hit a ball out of towering, triple-tiered Yankee Stadium. This drive landed three rows from the top of the upper deck in left field. If it had been 20 feet to the right, it would have sailed through the open space over the bull pen and out into the street.

The man who threw the pitch for that tremendous blast was the Yankees' Lefty Gomez, a man who developed real respect for Jimmy Foxx. After that game, Gomez took a long walk up into the stands to see where the ball hit. It had landed with such force that it shattered a seat, and years later, Gomez said, "I came to be proud to have a part in such a hit."

Another time when Gomez was pitching to Foxx, he shook off every sign that the catcher gave him. Finally, the catcher angrily came out to the pitcher's mound. "I've called for every pitch you use," he said. "What do you want to pitch to this guy?"

"To tell the truth," the zany pitcher replied, "I'd rather not pitch to him at all. I've been stalling out here hoping that he'd go away."

By the time Jimmy retired, he stood second only to Ruth in home runs with 534, and ranked third in slugging average, fourth in runs batted in, and fifth in extra base hits and total bases. Since his retirement, others have passed him on some of these lists, but he remains one of a handful that rank in the top

ten in every slugging category. Although he may
have been forgotten by many fans, his name still has
a big place in any baseball record book.

James Emory Foxx was born October 22, 1907, in
Sudlersville, Maryland. He was twelve years younger
than Babe Ruth and 21 years younger than Frank
"Home Run" Baker, who grew up in a nearby town.
Baker would play an important part in Foxx's career.

Jimmy was of Protestant Irish parentage. He grew
up on a farm, plowing the fields, pitching hay, milk-
ing cows, feeding the livestock. It was outdoors work
and he grew up husky and strong.

Jimmy's grandfather was a drummer boy in the
Confederate Army during the Civil War. It is said
that Jimmy ran away to join the Army when he was
only ten, but was refused and sent home. He turned
to sports, but first to track, rather than baseball.

"I dreamed of becoming faster than Charley Pad-
dock, who was 'the world's fastest human' at that
time," he once recalled. "I could run the hundred in
less than 10 seconds flat as a teenager and always
was faster than I looked later when I became big
and burly."

"Home Run" Baker first noticed Foxx in 1922
when he was a 160-pound 14-year-old who pitched
and played third base.

"I could see he had something special and was
worth watching," Baker recalled years later. He kept
track of Foxx, and in the summer of 1924, when
Baker was managing the Easton club of the Eastern
Shore League, he needed a catcher. It struck him
that young Jimmy, who was not yet 17, might be
able to do the job.

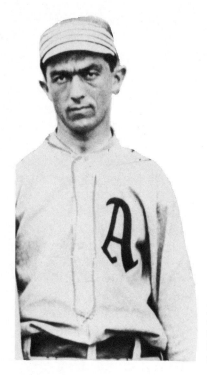

Frank "Home Run" Baker, who got his nickname by hitting two game-winning round-trippers in the 1911 World Series.

Foxx later recalled, "I received one of those old penny post cards signed 'Frank "Home Run" Baker,' which was a thrill by itself. He had scribbled on the back, 'Would you be interested in being a professional ballplayer?' I was only 16, but I sure was interested and I wrote him that."

The youngster went to Easton in his overalls to try out. Baker suggested that he try catching and Foxx took right to it. He caught 76 games for Easton and hit .296 with 10 home runs in the last half of the season. Even before the season was over, the Easton team needed money and Frank Baker was hoping to make a deal for Foxx. He spoke to his two former teams, the Yankees and Athletics, and both expressed interest in the 16-year-old.

Baker told Foxx that he had had offers from both the Yankees and the Athletics. He gave Jimmy the choice but recommended the A's because of their manager-owner Connie Mack.

Mack was already the grand old man of baseball. He had played in the majors from 1886 to 1896 and had taken over the management of the Athletics in 1901. From 1910 to 1914 the A's had won four pennants in five years, but then Mack was forced to sell off his stars and the team plummeted to last place. Now he was rebuilding again. Although he was already 62 years old, he would outlast Foxx and another whole generation of ballplayers, managing the A's through the 1950 season when he was 88 years old.

Foxx decided to take Baker's advice and accept the offer of Connie Mack's Athletics for the great salary of $2,000 a season. Foxx finished the season with Easton and then went on tour with a pick-up team. He was not planning to report to the A's until the following spring. But then one day in September, when he was playing in an all-star game in Martinsville, West Virginia, he received an order from Mack to report to the A's at once. So, before his 17th birthday, in September of 1924, Jimmy first went up to the big leagues.

He appeared in no games that season, but Mack had a good chance to take a look at him. Jimmy caught batting practice, took a few practice swings himself and sat next to Mack on the bench during the games.

Mack apparently saw some promise in Foxx's hit-

ting. But as a catcher, the young man had some real
competition. In the spring of 1925 a rookie catcher
named Mickey Cochrane came up to the A's. In his
first season Cochrane hit .331, and within a few
years he became one of the best catchers ever seen
in baseball.

Foxx opened the 1925 season on the A's major
league roster. That was a fine Philadelphia team,
whose star was Al Simmons, a .384 hitter. The 17-
year-old Foxx came up nine times as a pinch hitter
and caught a few innings, but then was sent back to
the minors. Although he got six hits in his nine at-
bats, he still wasn't ready for big league competition.
He was farmed out to Providence of the International League, where he hit .327 with one homer in
41 games.

In 1926 Foxx returned to the A's to remain. He
appeared in only 26 games that year, pinch hitting
and filling in as catcher. The A's finished third as
Ruth drove the Yankees to the pennant. In 1927, the
year Ruth hit 60 home runs, Foxx was still only 19.
By this time Mickey Cochrane was well-established
as the Athletics' catcher, and Foxx was used as a
spare at first base and as a pinch hitter. He got into
only 61 games but he batted .323 and hit three home
runs, his first in the majors.

In 1928 Foxx began playing more regularly. But
he was still a utility man, playing at first base, third
base and behind the plate. He hit a good .328 and
slammed 13 homers in 118 games. Late in the season
the A's got hot. They overcame a 13½ game Yankee
lead, moving into first place in September. But then
they faltered at the finish, losing the flag by 2½
games to the Yanks.

In 1929 Foxx was ready to become a star. He was 21 years old, and already he had spent three full seasons in the majors. The only question was, what position would he play? In spring training of 1929, he tried third base. Then just before the opener of the regular season, Connie Mack asked, "Do you have a first baseman's glove?" "No sir," Foxx replied. He had been borrowing a first baseman's glove whenever he filled in there.

Mack said, "Better buy one because you're our regular first baseman from now on."

So, after pitching, catching and playing third, Jimmy finally had a regular spot in the line-up. He soon became a better-than-average first baseman, but his fielding wasn't really what counted.

"My real position was at-bat," he once said with a smile.

In his first year as a regular, he hit .354 with 33 homers, 123 runs scored and 117 runs batted in. At the same time, Al Simmons, the Athletics' big slugger, hit .365 with 34 homers and 157 RBI's. George Earnshaw pitched 24 victories and Lefty Grove 20. The A's had a great season, winning 104 games and finishing 18 games ahead of the Yankees.

In that 1929 World Series, the A's opposed the Chicago Cubs, who also had their share of great hitters, including Rogers Hornsby and Hack Wilson.

Hornsby is sometimes considered the greatest percentage hitter of modern times. In three different seasons his average was over .400, and he finished his career with a lifetime average of .353—third highest of all time. Hornsby was a tough, outspoken man who was traded around the National League despite his potent bat. Although he was basically a percent-

age hitter, he had a slugging average of .756 one season, a higher mark than anyone except Ruth or
Gehrig ever achieved.

Hornsby's teammate, Hack Wilson, was a little
round man standing 5-foot-6 and weighing 200
pounds. He couldn't run well and he was a poor
fielder, but in his prime he was a top hitter. In 1929
he hit 39 homers. Then in 1930 he hit 56, setting a
National League record that still stands, and driving
in 190 runs, a major league record that may never be
broken. Unfortunately, Wilson was a heavy drinker,
and within a few years he disappeared from the
major leagues.

The 1929 Series between the A's and the Cubs
was a classic. In the first game, Connie Mack surprised the baseball world by starting Howard
Ehmke, who had pitched only 11 games in the regular season. Ehmke struck out 13 Cubs to set a Series
record which was to last nearly a quarter of a cen-
tury. Foxx hit a home run and a single to beat the
Chicagoans 3-1. The next day Foxx smashed a single,
double and a homer and drove home three runs as
the A's blasted the Cubs 9-3.

In Philadelphia in the third game, however, the
Cubs seemed to pull themselves together. They beat
the Athletics' star pitcher, George Earnshaw, 3-1. In
the fourth game the Cubs were sailing along with an
8-0 shutout when the A's came to bat in the last of
the seventh.

Simmons opened the inning with a homer. Foxx
singled and so did the next three batters. Then pinch
hitter George Burns popped up for the first out.
Then another single made the score 8-4 with two on.
The next batter was Mule Haas. He hit a long fly to

Jimmy Foxx comes home after hitting a three-run homer in the 1929 World Series.

center fielder Hack Wilson. The roly-poly slugger missed the ball and it went for an inside-the-park homer, making it 8-7. The next batter walked, Simmons singled, and Foxx singled again to drive home the tying run.

By now the Philadelphia fans were going wild and the high-flying Cubs seemed stunned. Their third pitcher of the inning came in and hit the first batter he faced to load the bases. Dykes then doubled to drive in two runs, putting the A's on top 10-8. The A's held on to their lead after putting together the most explosive inning in World Series history. The next day they finished off the Cubs to become World Champions.

Foxx hit .350 for the Series. In the winner's dressing room he smiled happily and said, "What a thrill. My first full season as a regular in the major leagues and I help my team win the world championship."

The following season produced an even greater thrill for Foxx, the one he came to call the greatest of his career. In the regular season he had hit .335 with 37 homers and 156 RBI's. Simmons had hit .381 with 36 homers and 165 RBI's, and Grove had won 28 games to lead the A's to their second straight pennant. In the World Series the A's faced the St. Louis Cardinals.

In the first game the Card pitcher was Burleigh Grimes, the last of the legal spit-ball pitchers. He moistened the ball with saliva and could make it do tricks that other pitchers couldn't manage. In the second inning Foxx stepped into one of Burleigh's spitters and slapped it off the right-field wall for a triple. But in the fifth Burleigh fooled him on a low spitter and he struck out. In the sixth Grimes had Foxx looking for a spitter and struck him out on a high curve. Although Foxx had been fooled, the A's won the game 5-2.

After four games, the Series was deadlocked at two games apiece, and the A's would be facing Burleigh Grimes again in the fifth game. Before the game Mack took Foxx aside. "Jimmy, you watch out for that pitch," he said. "He figures he has your number. And watch for that curve ball."

Foxx came up in the second and hit a fast ball for a long fly to left. In the fifth he swung on the first pitch and poked a single to center, but it didn't come to anything. Then in the seventh inning Grimes got Foxx in a one-and-two spot and threw a fast ball past him for the third strike. Foxx tells the rest of the story himself.

"In the ninth there was still no score. Each team had only three hits. Grimes was bearing down. He pitched too carefully to Cochrane, and Mickey got a free ticket to first. Simmons came up but he undercut a spitter and popped out. That brought me up again. I was nervous. Grimes was cool as a cucumber. He was deliberately slow in getting ready to pitch, so I stepped out. I got some dirt on my hands and stepped in.

"He raised his hand to his mouth in his spitter motion. Then he threw his first pitch. I knew in that flash second it wasn't a spitter for it was coming in close, like he threw his curve. I figured it for a curve, which it was, and I swung just right. Well, that was it. The big thrill. I heard the Athletics' bench yelling all at once and there it went. Some fan reached up and pulled it down when it hit in the left-field bleachers for a home run. It was a grand feeling, the thrill of a lifetime, and it lasted me forever."

Following that 2-0 triumph, the A's wrapped up the Series in the sixth game as George Earnshaw pitched a 7-1 victory. Foxx doubled and scored a run and finished with .333 on seven hits, including the big ninth inning home run off troublesome Burleigh Grimes.

Going into the 1931 season, Foxx signed a three-year contract for about $16,000 a season. The Great

Depression had made baseball fans and money
scarce, and even Babe Ruth had taken a cut in pay.
But Foxx was now the greatest slugger in the game
and others were earning twice or three times as
much. Foxx was always an agreeable sort and was
willing to take whatever salary was offered.

Foxx had a broad face, which seemed always to be
wreathed in a broad smile. He wore his dark hair
slicked back, and was handsome in a rugged way. He

Foxx poses with his great manager, Connie Mack.

was friendly, cooperative with the press and public, easy with fans and strangers. He was fond of scotch whiskey but never was famous for bad conduct off the field.

During the season he just played. In 1931 he hit .291 with 30 homers and 120 RBI's. For him this was a slump. Al Simmons had one of his best seasons, winning the batting title with a .390 average. Cochrane hit .349. Lefty Grove won 31 games and lost only four. The A's won 107 games and won the pennant by 14½ games from the Yankees. The season ended on a sour note, however, when the A's lost the World Series to the St. Louis Cardinals. Foxx batted .348, but the seventh game was won by his old pitching nemesis, Burleigh Grimes.

Foxx bounced back from his slump of 1931 to put together his best year in 1932. The Yankees captured the pennant by 13 games, dethroning the A's, but Foxx was a fury. Early in the season he was hitting homers at a faster pace than Babe Ruth's in 1927. Then he slumped in August. But going into the last two weeks of the season, he had collected 51 round-trippers and was threatening Ruth's record of 60.

On Sunday, the 11th of September, he hit his 52nd to give the A's a 5-4 victory in Detroit. But then the rest of the week went by without another. As each game passed, Jimmy's chances of hitting 60 got smaller.

He sat in the dressing room after one game that week, and told reporters with a sigh, "I'm just trying to hit the ball, fellows. I'm just trying to get my hits. I'm just trying to help the team win. If you try too hard for home runs, you usually don't get them. I'm feeling the pressure some, sure. The Babe is a big

man. His is a big record. I'm young yet. I hope I
make it, but if I don't, I hope I have other chances.
It's tough, you know. The pitchers aren't giving me
anything good."

On Sunday the 18th, the A's swept two from the
White Sox. Foxx revived hopes as he slammed his
53rd homer among three hits in the first game. He
settled for just two singles in the second. On Mon-
day, as Grove won his 25th and the A's won 9-6,
Foxx settled for one double in five tries, starting the
last week.

Tuesday was a day off. "Maybe I'd have hit a cou-
ple today," Foxx said wistfully. He was back home in
Philadelphia for the last five games and he needed
seven homers. The Philadelphia fans had no hope for
a pennant, but they came out to root for Foxx. On
Wednesday the Yankees and Ruth, himself, came to
town and Jimmy jolted Yank pitcher Red Ruffing for
his 54th of the year. It was also the 159th team
homer of the year, surpassing the league record of
158 set by the 1927 Yankees.

On Thursday the Yankees won 8-7 in 10 innings,
but Foxx hit a bases-loaded homer off Lefty Gomez
in the third and a solo blast off reliefer Wilcy Moore
in the seventh to reach 56. Both went over the right-
center-field wall and were real wallops. Ruth said,
"This kid isn't kidding."

On Friday the A's clinched second place by beating the Washington Senators 8-4, but Foxx couldn't
connect for the distance, though slamming a double
and single. On Saturday he hit his 57th, another
grand slam. He swung from the heels the rest of the
day, hoping to get another, but he could manage
only a single.

So it came down to the last day of the season with Foxx needing three homers to tie Ruth's record. He had a perfect day of sorts, with his 58th homer, two singles and a walk in four at-bats. But the one homer wasn't good enough. He had hit five homers in the last five days, but had to settle for 58. Disappointed but not depressed, Foxx said, "Well I gave her a ride to the finish, boys."

That he had. His .364 batting average was only three points behind the leader's. He led the league with his 58 homers, 151 runs scored and 169 batted in. Only Ruth and Roger Maris have ever hit more homers in a season, and Foxx's 169 RBI's, 100 extra-base hits, 438 total bases and .749 slugging average still rank in the top ten season totals ever. It was no wonder that while his side finished second, he was voted the league's Most Valuable Player.

An examination of his record that year revealed that he hit the screen in front of the left-field bleachers at Cleveland's League Park three times and hit the screen atop the left field fence in Sportsman's Park, St. Louis, five times. Neither of these screens were there in 1927 when Ruth hit 60. If playing conditions had been exactly the same, perhaps Foxx really would have broken the record.

In 1933 he won the Triple Crown, leading the league with a .356 batting average, 48 homers and 163 runs batted in. He also led the league with 94 extra-base hits, 403 total bases and a .703 slugging percentage. Though Philadelphia faded to third, Foxx was honored with his second straight Most Valuable Player award.

One day that season he hit four homers, two in each game in a doubleheader against the Browns in

St. Louis. He almost had six homers, narrowly missing with two 400-foot drives that hit near the top of
the fence, and went for a double and triple. Another
time he hit four homers in four at-bats, one the last
time up one game, three the first three times up the
next game.

Sadly, Connie Mack was having money trouble.
Times were not improving and he asked Foxx to take
a cut from his $16,000 salary to $12,000. "I had a

Foxx relaxes on the sidelines.

helluva time settling with the old man for my $16,000 again," laughed Foxx years later.

Once before, Mack had been forced to sell off his stars to stay in business. Now he had to do the same thing again. The great Mickey Cochrane went to Detroit and Lefty Grove went to Boston. But Mack held on to Jimmy Foxx—at least for the time being.

In 1934 and 1935 as Ruth slipped out of baseball, Foxx continued his slugging performances. In 1935 he helped win the All-Star Game with a long homer to left for two runs. But the A's slipped to fifth in 1934 then all the way into the cellar in 1935 and attendance in Philadelphia continued going down, too.

By this time, Jimmy Foxx was the last of Connie Mack's superstars. But in the winter of 1935 the old man had to sell him too. Foxx and a minor pitcher, John Marcum, went to the Boston Red Sox for $150,000 and two minor players. The fans in Philadelphia were frustrated. Twice Mack had stripped great teams of their greatest players. Never again would Philadelphia have a pennant contender.

In Boston, the owner of the Red Sox, millionaire Tom Yawkey, was trying to buy a pennant for the team. He had instructed his general manager, Eddie Collins, to buy up the best talent available. Many teams were in financial trouble and might sell good players for cash. Collins bought a player-manager, Joe Cronin, Lefty Grove of the A's, Rube Walberg, Wes Ferrell, Herb Pennock, Doc Cramer, Foxx and others. Later he began to buy promising prospects from the minors and obtained Ted Williams, Bobby Doerr, Dom DiMaggio, Johnny Pesky and others.

Foxx was 28 when he landed in Boston. The left-field fence in Fenway Park was only 315 feet away, a

tempting target for a powerful right-handed slugger.
He made good use of it, although he never approached his high of 58 homers in a season. His first
year with the Red Sox, Foxx averaged .338 and hit
41 homers and drove home 143 runs. In 1937 he fell
off to a .285 average, 36 homers and 127 RBI's, but
his third season, he put together one of his greatest
years with a .349 batting average, 50 home runs and
a league-leading 175 RBI's.

Foxx at this time was the greatest slugger in the
game. Ruth was gone and Gehrig was almost
finished. Other younger men were coming along—
Hank Greenberg, Joe DiMaggio and Ted Williams—
but Foxx was still on top. Yet he received little special attention.

Jimmy smiled wistfully one day and said, "I was
shadowed by Ruth. So was Gehrig. But the Bambino
was a fantastic hitter. And incredibly colorful. The
rest of us suffer by comparison. Some of us are pretty
good, too, but the Babe was just too good."

The only other slugger of Foxx's generation that
compared to him was Mel Ott, who played for the
New York Giants from 1926 to 1947. Like Foxx, he
was signed as a catcher at the age of 16, by the
Giants in 1925. The Giants' legendary manager,
John McGraw, soon recognized what he called, "the
greatest natural swing I've ever seen."

Ott made the majors the next year at the age of
17. McGraw put him in the outfield and he remained
there for more than two decades. A left-handed hitter, he would raise his right foot a foot off the ground
and stab forward with it just before he swung. At 5-
foot-9 and 170 pounds, he was not super-strong. But
his strong wrists and masterful timing gave him a

Mel Ott.

beautiful quick swing, and he mastered the art of lifting fly balls over the short right field fence in the Giants' home park, the Polo Grounds.

Master Melvin, as he was called, was more consistent than spectacular. He hit 42 home runs in his first full season and seven times he hit 30 or more. He drove in 100 or more runs nine times, with an

Hank Greenberg.

early-career season high of 151, and a career total of 1,860. His 511 career home runs make him one of eleven in the select circle with 500 or more.

In the late 1930s Hank Greenberg of the Tigers emerged as the foremost rival to Jimmy Foxx as a slugger. Greenberg was a great hitter. He drove in 170 runs in 1935 and 183 in 1937, the third highest mark in history. In 1937 he tied Foxx's 58 homers, becoming the third man ever to hit that many. After returning from the Army in the 1945 season, he hit a grand-slam home run in the last of the ninth inning of the last game of the season to win the game and put the Tigers in the World Series.

But Greenberg lost $3\frac{1}{2}$ seasons to the service during World War II and another half-year to a broken wrist while at his peak. After leading the league with 44 homers and 127 RBI's in 1946 at the age of 35, Greenberg was sold to the Pirates, had a poor season and retired.

At the end of the 1930s, Jimmy Foxx was still performing magnificently. In 1938 he was voted MVP for the third time, despite Greenberg's 58 homers. In 1939 Foxx hit only 35 homers and drove home only 105 RBI's, but he compiled a .360 batting average. He had a teammate on the Red Sox, a rookie named Ted Williams, who led the league with 145 RBI's and threatened to supplant him as the club's slugging leader.

Foxx said years later, "What a cocky kid that Ted Williams was. He thought he was the best before he had done anything. But he was bound to be one of the best, who would do almost everything before he was done."

Williams said, "I truly admired Foxx. He was older, of course, but a good-natured guy. Foxx was getting toward the end of his career, but he was hanging in, every once in a while really crashing one.

"I remember on a road trip that year Jimmy hit some balls like I had never seen before. The first one

was a real ripper in Chicago, over the left-field
bleachers. And in Cleveland, Foxx hit one over the
435-foot sign, at least 480 feet in the air. Then in Detroit he hit the longest ball I had ever seen—way up
into the bleachers in left center. Just hard to believe."

In 1940 Foxx's average slipped below .300, but he
still hit 36 homers and drove home 119 runs. It was
the twelfth consecutive season he had hit 30 or more
homers, a major league record. In May he tied a
major league record by hitting grand-slam homers in
two consecutive games. And in September he hit the
500th homer of his grand career.

The Red Sox, who had risen from the second division to second place in 1938 and 1939, fell to fourth
in 1940. They scrambled back to second in 1941, but
still were far behind the Yankees. And Foxx had become a part-time player, who hit only 19 home runs,
though he still managed to drive in 119 runs. How
the great sluggers could come through on aging legs!

In 1942, as the Red Sox finished a distant second
to the Yankees for the fourth time in five seasons,
Foxx was released on waivers to the Chicago Cubs in
June. He went to his manager, Joe Cronin, and said,
"Goodbye, Joe, and thanks for everything. And I
want to thank you especially for never asking me to
bunt."

Looking back on it, Cronin later said, "How could
you have asked a player with the power Jimmy Foxx
had to bunt?"

Cronin also felt Foxx might have been greater if
his personality had been different: "If Foxx had the
viciousness of a Ty Cobb he probably would have
bettered Babe Ruth's records. Well, now, I can't say

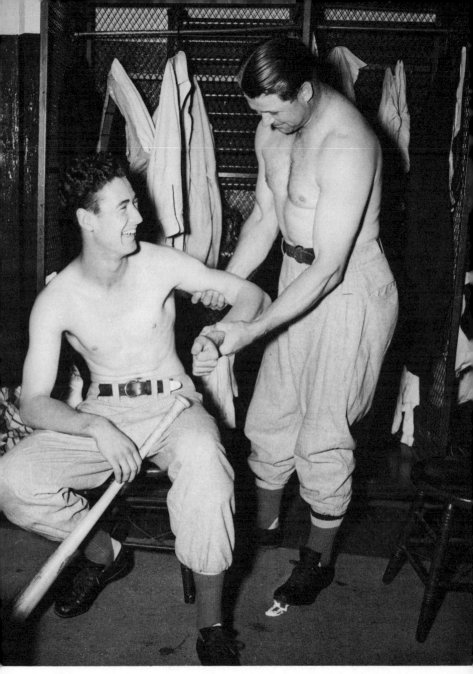

Muscular Jimmy Foxx teases his teammate, Ted Williams, about being so thin.

that for sure, but he wasn't driven by records. He had a cool disposition and he just played on sheer natural ability. He'd go out and have a few drinks at night and go out and play the game the next day. He liked to play. And he just played.

"He got hit in the head in an exhibition in Vancouver, a severe wallop, near the end of his career and he couldn't see so well after that. His last season with us he had cracked ribs. His legs were gone. We had to rebuild our team in an effort to catch the Yankees. We were good, but not good enough. I had to let Jimmy go. I hated to, but it was time, and he took it like a man."

Playing for Chicago, Foxx sadly admitted, "It looks like my slugging days are over now. I stand up there at the plate and feel great. I still have the power in my arms and wrists. My legs aren't too bad. But my eyes are bad. I can't see the ball real good any more."

He played poorly the last half of the 1942 season and retired and was out of baseball in 1943. But he'd spent all his money. "I was born to be broke," he once sighed. In 1944 World War II caused a great shortage of players. The Cubs called Foxx back, but it was no good. He got two hits in 20 tries, and they found him a managerial job at Portsmouth in the Piedmont League to finish up the season.

In 1945 he felt that his arm was still strong and that he might make it in the majors as a pitcher. He started two games for the Phillies and relieved in seven others, winning one, losing none, and recording a strong 1.57 earned run average. He even hit his last seven home runs, bringing his total to 534. But

Foxx was nearly 38 years old and was released by the Phillies.

Foxx managed a year at St. Petersburg in the Florida International League and a month at Bridgeport in the Colonial League and drifted from baseball in 1949. He was voted into the Hall of Fame in 1951, but otherwise lived in obscurity. He coached the University of Miami baseball team one year, but a bad back forced him to give that up. His business ventures failed and he declared bankruptcy. Tom Yawkey, owner of the Red Sox, gave him a job as coach of Boston's Minneapolis farm team in the American Association in 1958, but he couldn't hold on to it.

In 1963 he suffered a heart attack. His last years were dismal. His glories were long forgotten by 1967. He was hoping to attend the old-timers' reunion at the annual Hall of Fame ceremonies in Cooperstown in July that year. But a few days before, he was eating dinner with his brother when a piece of meat lodged in his throat and he choked to death. And so it ended for Old Double-X, the easygoing "beast" who terrorized pitchers for so long, the super-slugger few remember.

⚾ Ted Williams

Early in his career Ted Williams said, "All I want out of life is to become known as the greatest hitter who ever lived."

He came close to achieving his ambition. A few have hit for higher averages and a few have hit with more power, but very few batters have ever matched him for all-round hitting ability. When he retired in 1960, he had led the league four times in home runs, four times in runs batted in, six times in batting average and nine times in slugging average. His lifetime batting average, .344, was higher than that of any player since. At the same time, he hit 521 home runs (now eighth on the all-time list), even though his career was shortened by almost five full seasons of service in the armed forces.

During his major-league career, which stretched from 1939 to 1960, there were many other great players in the major leagues: Joe DiMaggio, Stan Musial, Willie Mays and Hank Aaron, to name a few. But none of them ever approached his performance

as an all-round hitter. And none of them approached him as a figure of controversy, either.

Williams always stood apart from others. He was outspoken, supersensitive, easily angered and usually the center of a storm of argument. He was one of the most dedicated students of the art of hitting who ever played the game, yet he was accused of not being so dedicated to his team and of choking up in crucial contests. Compared to Ruth and Foxx and many other stars, he lived a blameless life off the field. And yet through most of his career he was considered baseball's bad boy.

His most despised opponents (and perhaps the cause of some of his troubles) were the baseball writers. They sometimes seemed to criticize him no matter what he did. And in turn, he complained about them, refused to talk to them, cursed them and—on several occasions—spat in their direction.

Despite his great performances, he even had trouble with the fans. During his 19 seasons with the Boston Red Sox, the Boston fans seemed to love and hate him at the same time. They came to see him play—the other major league team in Boston, the Braves, couldn't compete with him and finally moved to Milwaukee. But the fans expected more of Ted than of ordinary players. They cheered him when he hit, but booed him when he missed. And he was sensitive to any hint of criticism. He once admitted that if there was one fan booing in a cheering crowd of 10,000, he would hear the boo. Early in his career he decided never to tip his hat to a crowd.

Ted Williams went his own way and did his own thing throughout his playing career. But in the end

he did it so well that his harshest critics had to admit
his greatness.

Williams was born August 30, 1918, in San Diego,
California, then a small town known mostly for its
navy base. On his birth certificate his name was
Teddy Samuel Williams, but he decided "Teddy"
was not dignified enough and changed his first name
to Theodore.

Ted's father had a photography shop in downtown
San Diego, and his mother was deeply involved in
the work of the Salvation Army. She marched
through the streets with their bands, collected
money and was even known by passers-by as "Salvation May." Unfortunately, she was so busy with her
religious work that she was seldom home to look
after her two sons.

When Ted was still a boy, his father abandoned
the family. This left Ted on his own even more and
he soon began devoting every spare minute to baseball. He was not close to his only brother and he
considered his mother over-religious. He wasn't interested in school, only in baseball. Near his home
was the North Park playground, which even had
lights for night play, and that's where Teddy could
be found most of the time.

From the very beginning, Ted Williams wanted to
be a hitter. He was asked to pitch at first and was
good at it, but he wasn't particularly interested. His
high school coach sometimes had to chase him
around the bases with a switch to get him to run full-
speed. When asked about this, Ted shrugged and
said, "I wasn't put on earth to steal bases."

The young slugger had a picture of Babe Ruth in his bedroom, but his real hero was Bill Terry, a first baseman for the New York Giants who had hit .401 in 1930. Terry was also outspoken off the field, and the young Williams admired him for that, too.

During his high school career, Ted pitched and played off-games at other positions. He hit .430 and by graduation, several major league teams were interested in him. His parents suddenly took an interest in his baseball and insisted that he get a $1,000 bonus. The St. Louis Cardinals offered only a few hundred dollars and the Yankees offered $500. Williams was only 17, but he and his family stuck to their $1,000 price. He finally signed with the local San Diego Padres, a minor league team in the Pacific Coast League, for $150 a month.

The manager of the Padres still thought that Ted was a pitcher. One day when the team was taking a beating, he sent his 17-year-old rookie to pinch hit for the pitcher and then stay in to pitch. Ted hit a double. Then he retired the first three batters to face him. But the next inning, the enemy batters began to hit his pitches all over the ballpark. When the manager came out to talk to him on the mound, the brash youngster suggested that anyone could see he was a better hitter than a pitcher and asked for a tryout in the outfield.

During the rest of the season he got into 42 games and hit .271. His performance broke no records, but was a fair showing for a boy who had just turned 18. The next season, 1937, he played regularly and hit .291 with 23 homers and 98 runs batted in. His record gave little indication that he would become the greatest hitter of his generation. Yet when Lefty

Young Ted Williams when he played for the minor league San Diego Padres.

O'Doul, a former major leaguer and manager of the San Francisco club, saw Ted at bat, he said, "There's the next Babe Ruth."

At this time the Boston Red Sox were still trying to assemble a pennant-winning team with the money of owner Tom Yawkey. A few years earlier they had bought Jimmy Foxx and several other established stars. Now they were scouting the minor leagues, looking for the most talented young players. They approached Williams and offered him a bonus of $1,000 and a two-year contract for $7,500 a year. Ted signed and was told to report to the Red Sox' spring training camp in 1938.

Soon after he arrived, Bobby Doerr, a stylish young second baseman, said to him, "Wait till you see Foxx hit!"

Williams answered, "Wait till Foxx sees *me* hit."

Although he was not yet 20, Williams acted as if he owned the team. On the first day of practice he went out to the field with his shirttail flying loose. Someone shouted, "Tuck your shirttail in, busher, this is the big leagues."

Williams turned to the man and told him that his shirttail was his own business. Later, when Ted asked who the man was, he learned that it was Joe Cronin, the Red Sox manager.

Ted made few friends. The veterans, especially the three regular outfielders, teased and taunted him. When Cronin finally decided that Ted needed another year in the minors, the outfielders, Chapman, Cramer and Vosmik, were there to wish him good riddance.

"I'll be back, you baboons," Williams said bitterly. "And someday I'll make more money than the three of you put together."

Then he went off to Minneapolis. But he would be back, and he would soon make good on his boast.

At Minneapolis he almost drove his manager, Donnie Bush, crazy. He would practice his batting stroke while in the outfield. Sometimes when a fly ball came his way, he would slap himself on the back-side and shout "Hi-yo, Silver," as he galloped off after it. Often he didn't catch it. When he struck out he would throw a temper tantrum, and if he hit a grounder he often wouldn't bother to run to first.

Finally the manager went to the team owner and said, "I can't take it any more. One of us has to go."

The owner smiled and said, "Don't be rash. If I have to choose between a manager and a .360 hitter, you can guess which one will have to go. Stick it out. He won't be with us long."

Williams would only be there the rest of the season. He led the league with a .366 batting average, 43 home runs, 142 runs batted in and 130 runs scored. The next spring he was called up to the Red Sox and Ben Chapman, the outfielder who had taunted him the year before, was traded to make room for him. Williams was not yet 21.

On Williams' first two times up in the majors, Yankee pitcher Red Ruffing struck him out on high fastballs. Jack Wilson, a teammate, needled Ted about it in the dugout, and Ted snapped that if Ruffing used the same pitch again, he would put it in the seats. He almost did what he promised, hitting a line drive that struck the wall a foot from the top and gaining his first major league hit.

Later that season Detroit catcher Rudy York tried needling the young Red Sox slugger. When Ted came to bat, the catcher said, "You're not hitting, are you, kid?"

"I sure as hell am," Williams replied. He hit the next pitch into the upper deck for a home run. And the next time up he became the first man ever to hit the ball completely out of the remodeled Briggs Stadium.

Williams started the season in right field. But he didn't like to play with the sun in his eyes, so he was

soon moved to left, where he played for the rest of
his career. He led the league's outfielders in errors
his first year with 19, and he would never become
more than an adequate fielder.

But his real interest was batting. "I was born to hit
a baseball," he said. He did 50 push-ups a day and
swung a 60-ounce bat for 30 minutes. He carried a
bat around with him and was always swinging it.
One time his roommate awoke suddenly early one
morning when Ted accidentally struck the bed post,
collapsing the bed with a crash.

"Boy, what power!" Williams said as his roommate struggled out of the ruins.

If he didn't have a bat with him, Ted swung an
imaginary bat—in bed, at the dining table, even in
the outfield. Every spring he took batting practice
until his hands blistered, bled and formed calluses.
Years later he sneered at modern batters who wore
gloves to protect their hands. "We don't have .400
hitters today because we don't have players who
want it enough," he said.

Williams had remarkable equipment for hitting a
baseball. Years later armed forces doctors tested his
vision and announced that only one person in
100,000 had eyesight as sharp. Pitchers, catchers and
umpires agreed that he could judge a pitch to within
a half-inch of the strike zone. And his reflexes allowed him to swing at the very last moment, seeming to hit the ball right out of the catcher's mitt.

But Williams always insisted that a large part of
his success was due to his desire. "It wasn't that I
saw better than other players," he said, "it was that I
looked harder, I was more intense."

He hit .327 his first season (well behind Foxx's

.360), but he led the league in runs batted in with 145 and hit 31 home runs. He was a sensation overnight and earned the nickname, "The Splendid Splinter," since he carried only 175 pounds on his 6-foot-4 frame.

In the 1940 season Ted batted .344, hitting 23 homers and driving in 113 runs. Yet the fans in Boston began to heckle him. Ted had been teased about an uncle who was a fireman, and one day he told a writer, "Nuts to baseball. I'd sooner be a fireman."

But his troubles seemed to intensify his desire to prove his ability. He entered the 1941 season with a deadly determination to establish himself as a superstar. He chipped an ankle in spring training and missed the first few games of the regular season. But he used the time to get in some extra batting practice.

His first game, he hit three singles and a homer. His second game, he hit a single and a double. In June he was hitting .436 and people began to take notice. But then another batting feat took the attention from Williams. Starting on May 15th, Joe DiMaggio of the Yankees had begun a hitting streak. By July 1 he had hit safely in 44 straight games, breaking the major league record. Baseball fans all over the country followed his progress day by day. By the time his streak ended at 56 on July 17, DiMaggio was a national hero.

This was the first of many occasions on which DiMaggio and Williams would be in competition. DiMaggio was four years older than Williams and had come up to the Yankees from San Francisco in 1936. His 56-game hitting streak remains one of the most amazing records in the book, and he had already shown himself to be a better all-round player than Williams. He was one of the most graceful and effective outfielders in history, and was an aggressive base runner as well as a fine hitter. In addition, his Yankees were pennant-winners or contenders almost every year. The argument about which was the better player may never be settled, but as the 1941 season wore on, Williams would show his talent at the plate.

In the same month that DiMaggio finished his hitting streak, Williams, still batting well over .400, hit a home run that he called "the biggest thrill of my career." The occasion was the All-Star game. Ted had doubled in a run in the fourth inning, but when he came up in the ninth, the American League was losing 5-4. There were two on and two out when Williams faced pitcher Claude Passeau of the Cubs. On a 2-1 count, Ted swung at a slider and drove the ball deep into the right-field seats to win the game.

As he saw the ball disappear, the young star began to jump and clap his hands. Then he literally danced around the bases, being met at home plate by Bob Feller and Joe DiMaggio. He was carried to the dressing room on the other players' shoulders and there was a tremendous celebration. "It was a wonderful, wonderful day," he said later.

Then Ted went back to the Red Sox and continued to bat at a .400 pace. Going into September, he was hitting .413. But the pressure was terrific and as season's end approached, he faltered. The Yankees had already won the pennant, so much of the attention of the league was focused on Williams and his average.

With two games left to go, Ted's average had

dropped to .39955—which would be rounded off to an even .400. If he stayed out of the final day's doubleheader, he would be assured of being the first .400 hitter since his old hero Bill Terry in 1930. Red Sox manager Joe Cronin urged him to sit it out, but Williams refused. "If I'm going to be a champion, I'll win like one," he said.

After a sleepless night, Ted stepped in to face pitcher Dick Fowler of the Philadelphia Athletics in the first inning. He singled. The next time up he hit a home run. Then against a relief pitcher he hit two

Williams is congratulated by Joe DiMaggio after his game-winning homer in the 1941 All Star game.

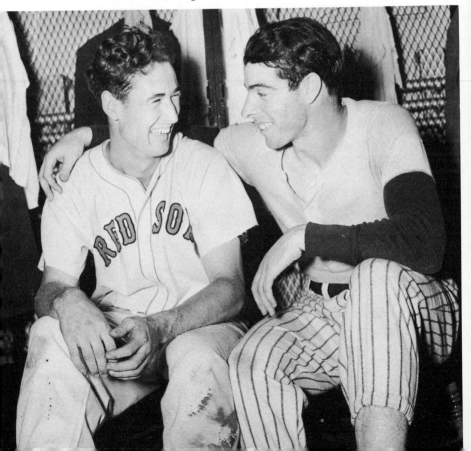

more singles—he had four hits in four at-bats. In the second game he got two more hits and raised his average to .406. It was a spectacular pressure performance—six hits in eight at-bats.

A month after his 23rd birthday, Ted Williams had become the first man in years to hit over .400. In addition, he led the league with 37 homers and a slugging average of .735—one of the ten best in history. He also drove in 120 runs, trailing the leader, Joe DiMaggio, by only five. In the years since 1941, it has been rare for batting leaders to come within 50 points of Williams' batting average *or* slugging average, and neither has been equaled.

But when the baseball writers met at the end of the season to vote for the American League's Most Valuable Player, they chose Joe DiMaggio. Ted was philosophical about the vote. "That's all right," he said. "He had a great year, a great streak, and *his* team won the pennant."

In December of 1941 the Japanese attacked Pearl Harbor, and the United States went to war against Japan and Germany. As the 1942 season started, more and more players were enlisting in the armed forces or were being drafted. Williams got a deferment on the ground that he provided the only support for his mother. Some fans and writers criticized him as unpatriotic.

But his play didn't seem to suffer. He won the Triple Crown, batting .356, hitting 36 homers and driving in 137 runs. He also led the league in slugging average (.645), runs scored (141), total bases (338) and walks (145). But the Yankees won the pennant again and their second baseman, Joe Gordon, was named Most Valuable Player. Ted's critics piped up again. If he were really a great player, they said, he would have led the Red Sox to the pennant. But it wasn't clear what more he could have done.

Before the 1943 season Ted went into the service. Apparently sensitive to the charges that he was a draft-dodger, he enlisted in the Marines and was assigned to flight training. After earning his wings, he was assigned to be a flight instructor and was never in combat. He missed the next three seasons as the war ended late in 1945. Meanwhile, the Red Sox finished seventh, fourth and seventh without him.

After missing what might have been his three greatest seasons, Ted returned to the Red Sox in 1946 determined to make up for lost time. In the opening game he faced another returning veteran, pitcher Lou Brissie, who had a metal plate in his leg. In the seventh inning Ted hit right back at Brissie and the ball clanged off his leg and knocked him down. Ted made it safely to first and then hurried to the mound with the other players to be sure that Brissie wasn't injured.

When Brissie saw Ted, he said, "For the love of Mike, Williams, why don't you pull the ball?"

Brissie stayed in the game and the next time up Williams hit a long homer down the right-field line. As he circled the bases, Brissie shouted, "You didn't have to pull it that far!"

The Red Sox were in contention for the pennant from the first of the season. Then in June came a new development that would plague Williams for the rest of his career.

On June 1 Ted hit three home runs, including a grand slammer, against the Cleveland Indians to give the Red Sox an 11-10 victory in the first game of a doubleheader. In the second game he doubled to right field with the bases loaded his first time up. When he came up a second time with no one on, the fielders had all changed position. Playing manager Lou Boudreau of the Indians had decided to challenge Ted's great pull-hitting to right field. The outfielders were all shifted far around toward right. The third baseman was playing in the normal shortstop position. Shortstop Boudreau was positioned to the right of second base, and the second baseman was midway between first and second.

"We can't field his home runs," Boudreau reasoned, "but if we tempt him to chop the ball to left we will cut down on his home runs and extra-base hits. If he hits into the shift and pulls the ball to right, we have a lot of fielders over there to take hits away from him."

This tactic became known as the "Boudreau shift" after its inventor. But it could as well have been called the "Williams shift." It was a controversial maneuver, and Williams' response to it was even more controversial. He almost always refused to chop the ball to left and stubbornly hit right into the crowded right side of the field. "They're trying to give me singles to left to take away my home runs to right and I won't let them do it," he insisted. Once again his critics questioned his judgment.

But the Red Sox were not to be stopped in 1946. They won 16 straight games at one point and finished twelve games ahead of the Tigers. Williams didn't lead the league in any major category, but he did hit .342 with 38 homers and 123 RBI's. And this year the baseball writers voted him Most Valuable Player in the league.

With Williams at bat, the Cardinals use the "Boudreau shift" in the 1946 World Series. Three infielders are playing between first and second base.

Three days before the World Series, Williams was hit in the elbow by a pitch during a warm-up game. Although it must have bothered him during the Series, he never mentioned it, and his critics had a field day when he batted only .200 as the Sox lost to the St. Louis Cardinals in seven games. Ted got only five singles and one of those was on a bunt. Now the Boston writers could claim that Williams choked up in crucial games, a charge which followed him to the end of his career.

It is not generally known that between the 1946 and 1947 seasons the Red Sox and the Yankees almost made the most spectacular baseball trade of all

time—Ted Williams for Joe DiMaggio. The rea-
soning was that each of the superstars was perfectly
suited to the other's home park. The right-handed
DiMaggio would become even more of a slugger
with the short left-field fence in Boston, and Williams would have the advantage of a short right field
in Yankee Stadium. The owners of the two clubs
shook hands on the deal, but then the Red Sox apparently got cold feet and asked for another player
along with DiMaggio—a rookie named Yogi Berra.
The Yankees refused and the deal fell through.

As it turned out, the Yankees would have gotten
the better side of the deal, since DiMaggio had only
five years to play and Williams didn't retire until
fourteen years later. Williams might have been paid
even more as a Yankee and gotten better support.
But he was a Red Sox hero (or goat) and he would
remain with them to the end of his career.

In 1947 Ted ignored the criticism and went back
to work at the plate. He won his second Triple
Crown, batting .343, hitting 32 homers and driving
in 114 runs. But the Red Sox slipped to third place
and the Yankees won the pennant again. In the MVP
voting, Williams lost by one point to Joe DiMaggio.
It was later revealed that one Boston writer did not
list Williams in the top ten for the award—if he had
put Williams even tenth, Ted would have won. Ted
claimed bitterly that the writers voted not for the
player who did most but for the player they liked
best.

One of Williams' eccentricities was his hatred of
neckties. Throughout his career he refused to wear
them on any occasion. When spring training opened

in 1948, the Red Sox had a new manager, Joe McCarthy, who had managed the Yankees for 15 years. He was a stern disciplinarian and a conservative dresser, and fans wondered how he would get along with Williams. On the first day of training, McCarthy came to dinner in an open-necked sport shirt—with no tie. When he was asked about his new style of dress, he said simply, "Anyone who can't get along with a .400 hitter is out of his mind."

The two men did get along fairly well, and Williams continued to compile amazing hitting statistics. He led the league with a .369 average, hit 25 homers and drove in 127 runs. The pennant race came down to the last day of the season and the regular schedule ended with the Red Sox and Lou Boudreau's Indians tied. The pennant-winner would be decided in a one-game playoff—another crucial contest for Williams. Once again he was the goat, managing to get only one single. Boudreau hit two singles and two homers as the Indians won 8-3 and went on to the World Series. According to the critics, Ted had choked up again.

In 1949 Williams turned 31 and was at the height of his powers. He won the Triple Crown for the third time, batting .343, hitting 43 homers and driving in 159 runs. Again the pennant race was a close one. The Red Sox led the Yankees by one game as they went into New York for the last two games of the season. New York won both contests and the pennant as Williams got only one hit (and four walks). Again he had failed in the crucial games, but at season's end he was named Most Valuable Player for the second time.

By this time Williams was not the brash kid who
had so offended the veterans in 1938. He had mel-
lowed somewhat, managing to get along with managers and teammates and to perform well despite
constant pressure from writers and fans. At the end
of the season, he disappeared—and spent most of his
off-time fishing. The quiet solitude of fishing seemed
to suit him almost as well as the batter's box. Still, he
was a prickly character. Some of his teammates re-
sented him and felt they couldn't count on him. And
managers had to watch their steps, too, since Ted
was more valuable to the team than they were.

By All-Star break in 1950, he was turning in another great season. But then at the All-Star game—

Williams comes to bat late in the 1953 season after serving nearly two
seasons in the Marine Corps.

the scene of some of his greatest moments—disaster struck. Chasing a fly ball in the first inning, he ran into the left-field wall at Chicago's Comiskey Park, injuring his elbow. Although he was in pain, he stayed in the game and singled in the leading run in the eighth. But the next day doctors discovered that there were 13 bone chips in his elbow and an operation would be required.

"They repaired the elbow as best they could," he said later, "but I was never the same hitter after that."

He played in only 89 games that season and hit only .317. The elbow continued to trouble him in 1951, and he hit only .318.

Then came another blow. The United States had gone to war in Korea in 1950, and just before the 1952 season Ted was recalled into the Marines. This time he complained bitterly. He felt he had already served and that he was being singled out because he was a celebrity. Again he was accused of being unpatriotic. But before he left, he hit .400 in six games. He was not discharged until late in the 1953 season, having missed nearly two full campaigns.

During his service in the Korean war, Williams did get into combat as a fighter pilot, and he nearly lost his life when he crash landed his burning plane. When he got out of the service, there was some doubt that he would return to baseball. He was within weeks of his 35th birthday, and he had been out of action for almost two seasons. Why should he endanger an already great career by playing when he was past his prime?

Then Branch Rickey, one of the great men of baseball, who had been general manager of the

Brooklyn Dodgers and other teams, met Williams by chance in an airport and helped convince the great slugger he should return. Ted's performance the closing weeks of the season was nothing short of spectacular. In 37 games he batted .407 and hit 13 home runs. If he had played a whole season at that clip, it would have been one of the greatest of all time.

In 1954 he cracked his collarbone and played in only 117 games. He hit .345 and lost the batting title because he did not have the required 400 times at bat. Even so, it was a disappointing season, and again he considered retirement. This time a fan approached him in a railroad station and pleaded with him not to quit. The fan pointed out that if he would only play a few more years, he could approach many lifetime major league records. Williams decided to continue playing, and whenever he approached a lifetime record, the fan would write him a note reminding him of the record and urging him on.

In the meantime, Ted's relations with the baseball writers were not improving. Several times after the writers had criticized him, he stood on the field and spat toward the press box. One time when he was being booed by the fans, he spat toward them, too, and was fined $5,000 by the Red Sox owner.

But he could always hit. He fought off a bad back, sore feet, a bout with pneumonia and advancing age. He had never been a great base runner and now running was harder than ever. "I always admired a Mickey Mantle or a Willie Mays," he once said. "They could get 35 or 40 leg hits a year, while I was lucky to beat out ten or twelve."

With or without leg hits, Ted continued to amaze.

In 1955 and 1956 he hit .356 and .345 although he lost the batting titles both years. Then in 1957 he hit .388, becoming at 39 the oldest player ever to win a batting title. He also hit 38 home runs, finishing second in the league. The next year he won the batting title again, although this time he hit only .328.

"If I didn't become the best hitter ever," he said, "I think I may have been the best old hitter of all time." Few would disagree.

But in 1959 it appeared that Williams' career was coming to an end. He suffered from a pinched nerve in his neck most of the year, and for the first time in 18 seasons he batted below .300. When the year was over, owner Tom Yawkey tried to talk Williams into retiring. But the Splendid Splinter was proud to the end and refused to finish his career with a .254 season. Although he was 41 years old, he insisted on returning for the 1960 season.

Ted started the season well and kept his average over .300 although he played in only about half the Red Sox' games. In July he appeared briefly in the All-Star game, but the American League was trounced 6-0, and one of the stars for the National League was Stan Musial, who was in many ways the National League's Ted Williams.

Musial was two years younger than Williams and had come up to the St. Louis Cardinals in 1941 when he was 20 years old. When he retired in 1963, Stan the Man had set some records of his own. He batted over .300 for 16 years in a row, leading the league six times. In 22 seasons (he missed one for service in the armed forces) he played in more games, came up to bat more times and got more hits than anyone except the great Ty Cobb. He ranked third of all time

Stan Musial and Williams chat before one of their many meetings in the All Star game.

in runs scored and runs batted in. Although he was not primarily a power hitter, he managed to hit 475 home runs as well. His lifetime batting average of .331 is second only to Williams' among all post-World War II players.

Musial even gave Williams competition as an "old hitter." In 1962, when he was 41 years old, Stan batted .330, third highest in the major leagues that year.

Unlike Williams, Musial had a strange, unorthodox stance and swing. But he also had much of the same natural equipment and desire. As the 1960s dawned, both Musial and Williams were nearing retirement, and baseball knew that their disappearance would mark the end of an era.

As the 1960 season came to an end, Ted Williams announced that it would be his last. The year had been miserable for the Red Sox as they finished seventh in their worst season since Williams arrived. But Ted was hitting well above .300 and had succeeded in redeeming his 1959 failures.

On the last day of the season, Williams was honored by the Boston fans in a ceremony before the game. Ted was never comfortable in these situations, but he took the microphone and said, "Despite the disagreeable things that have been said about me by the Knights of the Keyboard there in the press box, baseball has been the most wonderful thing in my life. If I were to start over again, I would want it to be in Boston with the greatest owner in baseball and the greatest fans in America."

He came up for the last time in the eighth inning against Baltimore pitcher Jack Fisher. It was a damp afternoon. The wind was blowing in toward the plate and it was getting dark. Fisher threw a fast ball and Ted swung and missed. But when Fisher threw a second fast ball, Ted swung and drove it into the bull pen in right-center field.

In all the years since 1942 he had never tipped his cap to the fans. Now, as he rounded the bases for the last time, he was tempted, but somehow he just couldn't do it. In the ninth he ran out to his position in left field and then was replaced by a substitute. As he ran off the field he received one more great ovation. It had been some career.

That last home run had been number 521, which still ranks eighth of all time. He had driven in 1,839 runs and gained a .634 slugging average, second only to Ruth's. But unlike other sluggers, Williams did

In a rare gesture, Williams tips his hat while being honored before his last game with the Red Sox.

not rank at the top of the all-time strike-out list. Mickey Mantle struck out more than 1,700 times, and Ruth and Foxx struck out more than 1,300. But Williams, a hitter's hitter, struck out only 709 times, while walking more than 2,000 times.

After that last game he was slow getting dressed. He talked easily with people in the dressing room, even writers. Finally he left, not to celebrate or get together with his teammates, but to go fishing.

In 1966 Williams was elected to the Hall of Fame and attended the induction ceremony without a tie. Then in 1969 he surprised the baseball world by signing on as manager (and part-owner) of the Washington Senators. The team moved to Texas in 1971. Ted showed some talent for managing—and especially for teaching hitting. But the team hovered near the cellar and Ted resigned after the 1972 season.

In July of 1969 the All-Star game was held in Washington, hosted by Williams' Senators. At that time a special banquet was scheduled to celebrate baseball's centennial year. Ted Williams was invited as a special guest. At the dinner the baseball commissioner was to announce the results of a poll to determine the greatest living baseball player.

But before the dinner was held, word leaked out that the honored player would be Joe DiMaggio. When the guests were seated, Joe DiMaggio was there. But Ted Williams wasn't. Proud even in retirement, the Splendid Splinter stayed home.

Willie Mays

Willie Mays was a great slugger, but above all, he was exciting. He burst onto the baseball scene in 1951, and almost immediately fans across the country were talking about him. How he could field! When he chased balls that would have been sure hits against any other outfielder, he could grab them while running directly at the outfield wall and then fire the ball to any base on one short bounce. When he ran the bases, he ran right out from under his cap, stretching his hits for extra bases.

And his hitting was even better. When Mays came to bat in the late innings and the game was close, the fans came to their feet. He would hit many a home run for the record book, but more important, he would hit to drive in the winning run or to score it himself.

Willie was excited about playing baseball and his excitement was contagious. Fans had idolized Babe Ruth and admired Ted Williams. Willie excited them. Unlike many other great sluggers, he also

seemed to inspire his teammates, and even in the last seasons of his long career, when he was tired and his performance was slipping, he never quite lost that enthusiasm for the game. By that time, he was a member of the small circle of all-time baseball heroes, ranking with Ruth, Foxx and Williams, the first member of his race to reach this height.

When Willie was a boy playing baseball in the sandlots near Birmingham, Alabama, the best a black ballplayer could look forward to was playing in the Negro Leagues. There were "major" Negro teams in most of the big cities of the East and the South, and they played to fairly large crowds. But compared to major league players, who were all white, Negro players led a hard life. They played more games for far less money; they traveled long distances, often in run-down buses, and stayed in second-rate hotels reserved for blacks only.

Perhaps most important, black players received no recognition outside the black community. Although some of the Negro League stars may have been among the best players ever to wear a uniform, they were unnoticed and they were kept out of competition with the great white stars of the major leagues.

Then in 1946, when Willie Mays was barely 15, the Brooklyn Dodgers announced that they had signed Jackie Robinson to play for their organization. He was the first black player to be admitted to "organized baseball." Suddenly, black ballplayers could dream of playing in the major leagues. For some, the change came too late. Such Negro League stars as Josh Gibson, Satchel Paige and Buck Leonard were too old to make good in the majors. Others, such as Robinson himself, Monte Irvin and

Roy Campanella, started major league play in the middle of their baseball careers.

But for Willie Mays, the change came just in time. He was one of the first generation of black players who played their whole professional careers in the majors. Soon Willie stood out above all the others, becoming one of the great all-round players and one of the greatest sluggers of any race.

He was born Willie Howard Mays, May 6, 1931, in Westfield, Alabama, and he grew up in Fairfield, near Birmingham.

Willie was his mother's first child. His father, a steel worker, divorced his mother when Willie was two years old, and Willie moved to Fairfield to live with his Aunt Sarah, his father's brother's widow.

Willie's mother remarried and had eleven other children, half-brothers and half-sisters to Willie. She died in childbirth in 1953 when Willie was 22. The next year, when Willie was a star for the New York Giants, his Aunt Sarah died.

Like many great players, Willie started as a pitcher. One day he pitched nine innings and won his own game with a home run. After touching home with the winning run, he collapsed. From then on he played full-time in the outfield. As his father said, it was better to be the one who hits the home run than the pitcher who gives it up.

Willie's dad, who had been a fine outfielder and hitter in the local black leagues, encouraged his son to play ball. "I was lucky," Willie once said, recalling his boyhood. "I didn't have to work much. My dad gave me walkin'-around money. He wanted me to be a ballplayer and he wanted me to have

time to become a good one. That's what I wanted,
too. It was all I was interested in. School didn't mean
much to me. It was just a place I had to go. I
dreamed of playing ball."

Although he dreamed of playing in black leagues,
the best that were open to him, his hero was the
great Yankee center fielder Joe DiMaggio. He tried
to copy the way Joe played the outfield and the way
he swung the bat. His hitting style became a close
copy of DiMaggio's, though he shortened Joe's un-
usually wide stance at the plate.

When Branch Rickey signed Jackie Robinson in
1946 and moved him up to the majors in 1947, a
whole new world of possibilities opened up to Willie
Mays. Robinson became one of his heroes and he im-
itated his daring, hustling style of play. Few people
had television then, but Mays may have seen Di-
Maggio and Robinson briefly in the newsreels at the
neighborhood movie house.

There were no organized leagues for the Negro
lads in small Southern towns in those days. But Willie played on pick-up teams—both hardball and softball. When he went to Fairfield Industrial High
School, the school did not even have a baseball
team, so he played basketball and football during the
school year. He took courses in dry cleaning and
pressing, which seemed like a likely occupation to
pursue for a lad in his place. One year he worked for
awhile washing dishes in a Birmingham cafe. Professional baseball seemed just a distant dream.

Mays was not big, but he was well-coordinated
and quick, and he became a fine basketball player in
high school. He led all players in black schools in his
county in scoring. He was an even better football

player, becoming a schoolboy passer of pro potential. In one game he threw eight touchdown passes. Some of his father's friends suggested that Willie apply for a scholarship to a black university so he could pursue his football. But both Willie and his dad preferred that he go after a baseball career.

So when Willie was 16, his father took him to Piper Davis, manager of the Birmingham Barons in the Negro National League for a tryout, and Willie showed enough promise to be offered a spot on the roster. He was still in school, but he was allowed to play in weekend home games until school let out. Then he toured with the club all summer. He was no sensation at the start, since he had to adjust to playing with older, more experienced performers, but he showed great natural talent.

Jack Hardy, a shortstop on an opposing team during Willie's first year, later recalled, "He made one throw on a runner coming home after a fly and it was a heller. We called him lucky and every other name in the book. Willie, he didn't say nothing. He just went out there next inning and made a better throw on a faster runner. We just kept our mouths shut after that."

Touring with the Barons, Willie got to play in the major league ballparks, including Sportsman's Park in St. Louis and the Polo Grounds in New York. On an off-day in St. Louis he went to Sportsman's Park and saw his first major league game, the Red Sox against the St. Louis Browns. He was awed by Ted Williams, and admitted years later, "I just sat there with my mouth open."

Later, Roy Campanella, then a star in the black leagues, took him barnstorming with other black

Mays poses with Dodger great Roy Campanella shortly after Willie joined the Giants.

stars, such as Monte Irvin and Hank Thompson. At 17, Mays batted against the immortal Satchel Paige and got one hit in two attempts. Major league scouts had plenty of opportunities to see him as he developed, but teams were still not actively scouting black players.

By 1950, Roy Campanella, Monte Irvin and Hank Thompson were playing in the major leagues—Campy for the Brooklyn Dodgers and Irvin and Thompson for the New York Giants. Willie Mays, who was still only 19, still hadn't been noticed. Then the New York Giants sent scout Eddie Montague to look at the Birmingham Barons' first baseman, Alonzo Perry. In the game Montague saw, Mays made great catches and throws. He also doubled off the right field wall, flied out deep to left, doubled to center, beat out a grounder and stole second and third.

Montague forgot all about Perry. He later recalled, "Once I saw Mays, it was hard to look at anyone else. He had quick hands, a great arm, hit line drives with power to all fields and was a jack rabbit on the bases. Here was a kid who had everything."

Montague hustled to a telephone, awakened his boss in New York and said he had spotted someone they had to sign. Perry was all right, but the important one was Willie Mays. He might make the majors within two years.

Why hadn't anyone spotted him before? Montague didn't know, but it was said that the Braves, the White Sox and the Yankees had been looking him over.

Montague was told to find out how much Mays would cost, watch him play once more and then sign him if the price was right. The Barons' owner told

Montague that Mays would cost $15,000. But it turned out that the Barons had no written contract with Mays, so the young man was a free agent.

When Montague visited Mays at his Aunt Sarah's, Willie was so excited he could hardly speak. Aunt Sarah was calmer. She said "her baby" ought to get at least $5,000 for signing.

Montague watched Willie in another game and was even more impressed. He also saw the Braves' scout again and began to grow nervous. He went to Mays' home immediately after the game, shared the family's fried chicken dinner and got Willie to sign a contract calling for a $5,000 bonus.

The Giants sent Willie a check for $5,000 and decided to send a check for $10,000 to the Barons so that there would be no doubt about the Giants' rights to the player. The Barons accepted the fee.

So, at 19 years old, Willie was assigned to Trenton, New Jersey, in a Class B minor league.

He arrived in the middle of the 1950 season nervous and frightened. It was not his first trip outside the South—he had traveled with the Barons. But this was different. For the first time he would be playing with white teammates, white managers and white opponents. In his first 22 at-bats he failed to get a hit. He went to his manager, Bill McKechnie, Jr., and said he doubted he had the ability to hit this pitching. The manager told him to relax and just keep swinging.

Willie got a hit the next time up and hit consistently the rest of the way. Even with a slow start, he finished the season with a remarkable .353 average in 81 games. Surprisingly, he hit only four home runs.

The next spring Willie trained with the Minneapolis Millers, the Giants' top minor league team. The Minneapolis camp was right next to the Giants' camp, and Giant manager Leo Durocher made a point to take a look at Willie himself. There is something about a great natural athlete that a professional can spot right away. Leo was enormously impressed by Mays' play. And when he met Willie in the dressing room, he took an immediate liking to the shy, but enthusiastic youngster.

Willie had a great future in the majors, but he wasn't ready yet. He started the 1951 season with Minneapolis and it looked as if he was going to tear the Triple-A American Association apart. In the first 35 games he averaged .477, hit eight homers, scored 38 runs and drove home 30.

Meanwhile in New York, the Giants got off to an extremely slow start. They lost ten straight in the first two weeks. Near the end of May they were in fifth place in the eight-team league, with 17 wins and 19 losses. Manager Durocher knew the team needed something extra. He had been receiving reports on Willie's great performances at Minneapolis, and he decided to bring the youngster up. Giant owner Horace Stoneham opposed the move—Willie was still too inexperienced, he said. But he reluctantly gave Leo permission to recall the prize prospect. In order to soften the blow in Minneapolis, where fans were counting on Willie, the Giants took out ads in the Minneapolis newspapers, apologizing to the fans for taking Mays away from them so soon.

"I don't know how I knew the kid was ready, but I knew," Durocher once said. "When you've been in this business as long as I have, you know. Sure, it might take time for him to adjust, but we had time, we weren't going anywhere without him, and I figured when he found himself we could go all the way with him. I figured he'd learn more playing against the best in the majors than against the players in the minors. I figured with his kind of ability he could learn fast. I took a chance. That's what life is, taking a chance."

"I was scared to death," Mays later recalled. "When they put Mr. Durocher on the phone to talk to me, I told him that I didn't think I was ready. But he said he thought I was. He said he knew more than me and he talked me into it."

So at 20, early in his second season as a pro, with less than one full season in the minors, Mays reported to the Giants in Philadelphia as they started a three-game series with the Phillies. Durocher put him right in the regular line-up, in center field. The big hitter for the Giants was Monte Irvin, another black player who had gone barnstorming with Mays a few years earlier. Soon the regular outfield for the Giants was Irvin, Mays and Don Mueller.

Mays went hitless in five trips his first game. He went hitless in three tries his second game, although he walked twice. He went hitless in four tries his third game. He was 0-for-12 when he returned with the team to New York to open a series with the Boston Braves in the Polo Grounds and he was worried. The newspapers were already comparing him to the great center fielders of the other New York teams. The Dodgers had Duke Snider, a fine hitter and fielder, and the Yankees had veteran Joe DiMaggio and a tremendously promising rookie named Mickey

Mantle. When Mays failed to hit in his first games, the writers and fans began wondering if Mays might be a dud.

In his first time at bat in the Polo Grounds in New York, Mays faced the brilliant left-hander Warren Spahn. On the first pitch, he guessed fast ball, swung, and drove the ball over the left-field roof for his first hit and his first home run. The home fans came to their feet to cheer him and his teammates greeted him at the dugout with enthusiasm. "It was a great thrill, a moment I'll never forget," he recalled.

But he then went hitless in his next 13 tries. And at 1-for-26 he was losing confidence. He went to Durocher and asked the manager to return him to the minor leagues. It was too much for him up here, he said. He wasn't ready. Maybe next year.

Leo told him he wasn't going anywhere, he was staying in center field, even if he didn't get a hit the rest of the year. Just keep swinging, Leo said, and you'll make it. Willie agreed to keep trying.

His next time up, he singled in a game against Pittsburgh. Then he tripled. Then he hit two doubles in a game against the Cardinals. Then he hit his second home run in a game against Cincinnati. On a Western tour late in June, he hit in ten straight games, slamming four homers and driving in 16 runs. He won a game in Chicago with a three-run homer in the tenth. He tied a game in Philadelphia with a homer in the ninth.

He wasn't tearing the majors apart, but he was beginning to hit consistently and was gaining confidence. Already he played with tremendous zest. He

Willie steals home against the Cubs during the Giants' 1951 drive to the pennant.

made some great plays in the outfield, and the rest of the team seemed taken by his spirit and hustle and boyish good nature.

The Giants had started to win with fair consistency, and had moved up to second place. But on August 11 after they lost a single game to Philadelphia, and after Brooklyn split a double header with Boston, the Dodgers led the Giants by 13 games with only 44 games to play.

Then the Giants started to streak. They won three straight from Philadelphia. Willie saved one game with a diving shoestring catch. Then they met the Dodgers in a three-game series in the Polo Grounds.

They won the first game and were tied 1-1 in the eighth inning of the second game with the Dodgers up. With Billy Cox on third and one out, Dodger outfielder Carl Furillo came to bat. Furillo was a right-handed pull hitter, but he drove the ball to deep right-center field. It seemed certain it would go for extra bases, breaking up the game. Mays, who had been standing in left-center, sprinted to his left and back toward the wall. Going at full speed, he reached his glove hand across his body and snared the ball. He then stopped dead, pivoted completely around on his left foot, and threw toward home.

The baserunner, Billy Cox, had stayed close to third, and when Mays made his amazing catch, Cox tagged up and took off for home. But the throw was perfect, reaching catcher Wes Westrum on one bounce. Cox was out and the inning was over.

"It was the perfectest throw I ever made," Mays said. Many who were there say it was the greatest single fielding play they ever saw.

Mays finished the game by singling and then scoring the winning run when Westrum homered. The next day Giant pitching ace Sal Maglie stopped the Dodgers, and the Giants had swept the series.

They kept winning until they had 16 straight games. Now they were only five games behind the Dodgers. At one point in August, Mays scattered six hits over several games—all home runs. Through the stretch run in September, the Dodgers gave ground grudgingly, but the Giants kept closing in. On the final Friday of the season, with two games left to play, they tied for first.

Both teams won on Saturday. Then the Giants won on Sunday. As outfielder Monte Irvin was waiting for the fly ball that would be the final out, Willie ran up to him and shouted, "If you drop it, I'll kill you!" He was excited beyond belief. Then he ran with the others to the dressing room to listen to the finish of the Dodger game in Philadelphia. If the Dodgers lost, the Giants would have the pennant.

The Dodgers had been behind 6-1, but had tied the game, and it went into extra innings. The Phillies loaded the bases with none out in the twelfth, but Jackie Robinson made a dramatic diving catch of a liner to save the game. Then, in the 14th inning, Robinson hit a home run to win the game. Now the National League pennant would be decided in a best-of-three playoff.

The Giants won the playoff opener 3-1, but the Dodgers came back to trounce the Giants 10-0 in the second game. Then in the third game the Dodgers took a 4-1 lead into the last of the ninth inning.

Durocher wasn't giving up, however. "Well, you've come this far," he said, "and you've still got a chance."

Alvin Dark led off for the Giants with a single and Don Mueller followed with another. Monte Irvin popped up for the first out, but then Whitey Lockman sliced a double to left, scoring a run. Now it was 4-2. Bobby Thomson was up with two men on, and young Willie Mays was on deck.

But Mays never came to bat. With the count no balls and one strike, Bobby Thomson swung and connected. The thousands of fans listening to Giant broadcaster Russ Hodges heard his voice raise in pitch as he said, "There's a long drive . . . it's gonna be . . . I believe . . . the Giants win the pennant! . . . Bobby hit the ball into the lower deck of the left-field stands! The Giants win the pennant and they're going crazy! I don't believe it. I don't believe it. I *do not* believe it. *Whooooeeee!*"

Willie Mays, who was waiting to be the next man at bat, said later, "It was my greatest thrill in baseball. That home run excited me more than any I ever hit myself."

That ninth-inning blast gave the Giants a 5-4 victory and the pennant. It was Thomson's 32nd homer and gave him 101 RBI's for the season. Monte Irvin had batted .312 and driven in 124 runs, to lead the club. Willie hit a respectable .274, hit 20 homers and drove in 68 runs in 121 games. He was not the leader of the team, but everyone agreed he was one of its sparkplugs.

In the World Series, Willie played against his old hero, Joe DiMaggio, for the first and only time—DiMaggio retired at the end of the season. Mickey Mantle, who had spent part of the season in the minors, got only one hit before he suffered the first of his many tragic injuries, damaging his knee in a fall in the outfield. Of the three great center fielders, DiMaggio was the one who came through. The Yankee Clipper got six hits, including a game-winning homer, as the Yanks won in six games. Willie batted .182, getting only four singles.

Giant hopes for Willie were postponed when he

Mays (upper center) is in the crowd greeting Bobby Thomson as he comes home with the pennant-winning run in 1951.

was drafted into the army before the 1952 season. He played in only 34 games and hit only .236 before leaving. The Giants finished second to the Dodgers in 1952 and slid all the way to fifth in 1953. Meanwhile, Willie played baseball and basketball for service teams and looked forward to returning to the Giants.

Never an enormous, muscular man like Foxx, nor a tall, rangy one like Williams, Mays was compact, quick and strong. He was 5-foot-11 and played at 185 pounds. He swung freely and he had great natural reflexes and timing. He studied pitchers, but he was more a natural player than a studious one. He seemed to make the right moves in the field by instinct. Baseball men had shuddered in 1951 when he made his famous basket catches, holding his glove below his waist to snare fly balls, but he knew what he was doing and he seldom made mistakes.

When Willie walked into the Giants' pre-season camp in the spring of 1954, he was welcomed as a returning hero. The Giants had finished 35 games out of first place the season before, and Leo Durocher hoped that Willie could give the team a boost as he had in 1951.

The baseball world soon knew that number 24 was back. He made great plays in the field, swung the bat with abandon and ran the bases with daring. He hit a home run in his first time up in spring training. On the opening day of the season he hit a 440-foot home run to beat the Dodgers. He hit a two-run homer to win the next game, too. Later he hit four home runs in a three-game sweep of the Dodgers.

He hit home runs in his first time up in five consecutive games. He hit a home run in the 14th inning

to beat the Cubs at Wrigley Field. He hit perhaps
the longest home run of his career, a 600-foot smash
into the upper deck in left field in Sportsman's Park,
St. Louis. When the season was over, he led the league with 41 homers and a .667 slugging percentage
and had driven home 110 runs.

On the last day of the season Willie was tied for
the batting title with teammate Don Mueller and
Dodger Duke Snider. In his last game the Duke was
shut out. Mueller got two hits, but Mays got three to
finish with a league-leading .345. The Giants had a
great year, finishing the season five games ahead of
the league. Willie was voted Most Valuable Player in
the National League and Player of the Year by *The
Sporting News.*

For the first time in six seasons, the New York
Yankees had failed to win the American League pennant. A great Cleveland team had won 111 games,
led by a great pitching staff and a black center
fielder named Larry Doby, who had led the league
in homers and RBI's. The World Series between the
Giants and the Indians opened at the Polo Grounds
on September 29th.

The first game was a pitchers' duel between the
Indians' Bob Lemon and the Giants' Sal Maglie. The
score was tied 2-2 in the top of the eighth inning
when the Indians put two men on with no outs.
Their next batter was Vic Wertz, who had driven in
the Indians' two runs with a triple in the first inning.
Now Wertz really connected with the ball, sending a
drive to center field that would have been a home
run in other parks. But at the Polo Grounds, the center-field wall was more than 460 feet away.

At the crack of the bat, Willie Mays whirled and

sprinted straight at the stands. Near the 460-foot mark, without even looking over his shoulder, he stretched out his glove and the ball sailed into it. Then he stopped, turned and fired a perfect throw to the infield, forcing the startled base runners to hold.

His back to the plate, Mays outraces Vic Wertz's drive in the 1954 World Series.

It was his most famous catch and it stole the game from the Indians. In the tenth inning the Giants' Dusty Rhodes came up as a pinch-hitter and slammed a three-run homer to win the game. After that the Indians folded, and the Giants swept the Series in four straight games. Rhodes was the hitting hero, but Willie had four hits, four runs scored and three runs batted in in the four games.

When he was asked about the catch later, he grinned and said, "It was one of my best, no doubt about that."

In New York Willie was a celebrity. He lived in Harlem, and when he wasn't playing for the Giants, he was playing stickball in the streets. Once Leo Durocher visited Willie and found his valuable star playing stickball between the parked cars. He asked him to stop, but Willie said, "Why? It isn't dark yet."

As the 1955 season approached, Willie turned 24. He was still young and filled with enthusiasm, and he had one of his best seasons. He hit 51 homers to lead the league, drove in 127 runs and batted .319. In the field, he led all outfielders in assists with 23. He also stole 24 bases, one less than the league leader.

But the Giants didn't do as well. They finished in third place, 18½ games behind the Dodgers. Then in a startling move, Giant owner Horace Stoneham dismissed Leo Durocher and appointed former Giant infielder Bill Rigney to take his place as manager. Willie and Leo had been almost like father and son, and Leo's departure seemed to diminish Mays' enthusiasm for the game.

In 1956 and 1957 Willie still played well, but some of the old spark was gone. New York finished both seasons in sixth place, losing more games than it won. Willie hit 36 and 35 home runs, and hit .296 and .333, but he failed to drive in 100 runs in either season. Still, he managed to lead the league both years in stolen bases with 40 and 38, a remarkable accomplishment among power hitters, who are usually big and slow on their feet.

A hero in his neighborhood near the Polo Grounds, Willie gets a taste of ice cream from a young fan.

Then at the end of the 1957 season there was another surprise. The Giants announced that the team was moving from New York to San Francisco. (At the same time, the Dodgers were moving to Los Angeles.) Willie had grown to love New York and the fans there loved him, too. It was sad for them to be separated.

Willie's reception in San Francisco was not as warm as expected. During the Giants' first season there, the crowds took to rookie Orlando Cepeda, but expected Mays to be spectacular as a matter of course. The team played in old Seals Stadium, which was so small that Willie's far-ranging fielding was frustrated. Otherwise he had a fairly good year, batting .347 and leading the league in stolen bases for the third year in a row. His home run production dropped to 29, however, and for the third year in a row he failed to drive in 100 runs. The Giants moved up from sixth place to third, but they weren't really in contention for the pennant.

The 1959 season was a heartbreaker for the Giants. With eight games to go, they led the league by two games. But the team fell into a sudden slump and finished in third place. Some of the fans blamed Mays.

"I don't know what these people want," he said. "I just do the best I can."

Despite his troubles, Mays was acknowledged as one of the great stars in baseball. It no longer seemed strange that a black player could be a superstar. But in 1960 fans were reminded that even a superstar had certain troubles if he was black. When Willie tried to buy a home in an exclusive suburb of San Francisco, vandals broke the windows and made it clear that he would not be welcome there. He later bought another home in a different area.

In 1960 he batted .319, led the league with 190 hits and stole 25 bases. But he was swinging more for hits than for home runs and again he hit only 29. The next season, he turned 30, and as he began to lose his speed he began to make up for it by hitting for power. He hit 40 home runs and drove in 123 runs, his highest totals since 1955. The Giants, who had finished fifth in 1960, had changed managers and under Al Dark, a former Giant star, they finished a close third in 1961.

On his first time up in the 1962 season, Mays hit a home run off the great Warren Spahn. It was a good sign. Willie was swinging for the fences, and a few days later he beat the New York Mets with home runs in the eighth and tenth innings. The rest of the team pulled together, too, and by September they were running neck-and-neck with the Dodgers for the pennant.

Then one day Willie collapsed in the dugout. He spent a few days in the hospital and doctors concluded that his dizzy spell had been caused by tension and exhaustion. After missing four games, he came back to tie his first game with a home run. The next day he hit another to win the game. Then on the last day of the season he hit a homer in the last of the eighth to give the Giants a 2-1 victory over Houston and tie them with the Dodgers.

Now the Giants faced another three-game playoff against the Dodgers. The Giants won the first game 8-0 as Willie collected two homers, a single and a walk in four times up. But in the second game the Giants blew a 5-0 lead and lost.

The third game was played in Dodger Stadium in Los Angeles. When the Giants came to bat in the top of the ninth, they were trailing 4-2—an eerie repetition of the situation in 1951. This time Mays came to bat with the bases loaded and one out. He slammed a drive back at the pitcher and it bounced off his leg, going for a single and scoring one run.

The second Giant hero, Orlando Cepeda, came up and hit a long fly. The runner on third scored the tying run after the catch. Then a walk and an error brought home two more runs to give the Giants a 6-4 lead. They held in the bottom of the ninth and, just as they had in 1951, they won the pennant playoff.

Finally, the fans in San Francisco were warming up to Willie. He had had a great season, batting .304 with 49 homers and 141 RBI's. In the World Series however, Willie batted only .250 as the Giants faced the New York Yankees. The contest went down to the last inning of the seventh game. The Giants came up trailing 1-0. With two out and a man on first, Willie Mays came through with a double, putting men on second and third. Then Willie McCovey smashed a hard line drive that might have won the game and the Series. But shortstop Bobby Richardson made a miraculous catch to save the victory for the Yankees. It was a disappointment for Giant fans, but 1962 had been a banner year anyway.

During the next two years the Giants sagged again, but Willie had two of his best seasons. He hit 38 homers and batted .314 in 1963, then led the league with 47 homers in 1964. Now he was earning over $100,000 a year, and in 1964 he was made captain of the team.

When a writer teasingly asked him where his captain's bars were, Willie replied, "You're trying to make fun of this, but I'm proud of it!"

Sadly, his pride in being captain was diminished late in the season when manager Al Dark was quoted in a newspaper as saying that the team was in trouble because it had too many black and Latin players. Dark suggested that such players were not as alert mentally or as proud as white players. Willie defended Dark in public, but never spoke to him again in private. At the end of the season Dark was fired.

The new manager, Herman Franks, reappointed Mays as captain and gave him additional responsibilities working with young players. In 1965 he had his last great season, slamming 52 homers and batting .317. In the process he hit his 500th homer late in the season.

One night after the 500th, he came up in the ninth inning with two out, a man on and the Giants behind by two runs. Houston pitcher Claude Raymond decided to get the great slugger on fast balls, and he threw ten of them in a row. Mays missed the first two for strikes, took the next three for balls and then fouled off four in a row. But on the tenth pitch, he swung and connected, driving the ball into the left-field stands and tying the game.

Teammate Len Gabrielson said afterward, "That was the greatest thing I ever saw. Everybody knew he needed a homer. He just went and got it."

Early in 1966 Mays approached Mel Ott's National League record of 511 home runs. Going into a doubleheader in Houston, he needed two to tie the record. He got one in the first game and then tied the second game with another.

After the game a writer asked him if he was thinking about tying the record. Willie said no. "What were you thinking of?" the writer asked.

"Tie game." Willie answered.

Ten days later Mays passed Ott's record with a homer at home against the Dodgers. As he circled the bases, the crowd cheered and applauded. After he entered the dugout, they chanted, "We want Willie!" until he came out and tipped his cap again.

Before the season was over, Willie had passed Ted Williams and early in 1967 he passed Jimmy Foxx to become the second greatest home run hitter next to Ruth. When someone asked if he might catch up to

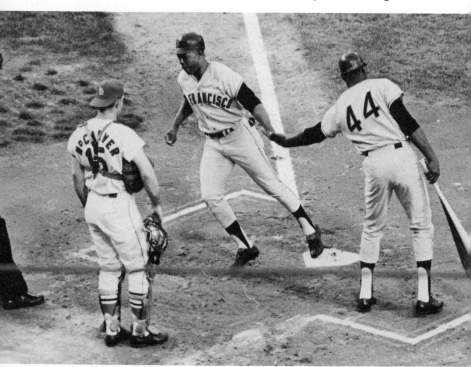

Willie scores after hitting his 522nd homer to pass Ted Williams on the all-time list.

the Babe's record, Willie laughed and said, "That man's in a league all by himself."

His 1967 season was the least productive since he came up to the majors. He hit only 22 homers and batted only .263. Willie was 36 and beginning to feel his age. But he insisted that he wanted to play for years to come. In 1968 he did about the same, and the Giants finished second for the fourth year in a row.

At the end of the 1968 season, Mickey Mantle retired. Of all the players in Willie's generation, only Mantle and Hank Aaron could approach his accomplishments. Mantle was six months younger than Willie, but he had been plagued throughout his career by serious injuries. Like Mays, Mantle was an exciting and inspirational player. He was voted Most Valuable Player in the American League three times and during the early part of his career the Yankees won the pennant more often than not.

Mickey completed his career with 536 home runs, two more than Jimmy Foxx, and a lifetime batting average of .298. In 1961 he had hit 54 homers, but had been eclipsed by his teammate, Roger Maris, who hit 61 that year, to break Babe Ruth's season record. Maris himself never reached the ranks of the great sluggers. Despite his one great year, he averaged fewer than 25 homers a season during a 12-year career.

From 1969 on, Willie Mays found it harder and harder to keep going. Herman Franks had been replaced as manager of the Giants, and the new managers found it harder to get along with Willie. In 1969 Willie hit only 13 homers, but one of those was the 600th of his career, putting him far ahead of all sluggers past and present except Hank Aaron and Ruth.

Some criticized him for continuing to play past his prime. But he replied, "No one knows when it's time for me to quit. I get tired these nights. I can't go like I used to go. But I still can sometimes. I can still help a team."

In 1970 he hit 28 homers, making it the 17th year that he had hit more than 20. In 1971 he hit only 18 as the Giants won the Western Division title in the newly divided National League. They disappointed their fans by losing in the playoffs to the Pirates in four games. Old man Mays had contributed four hits—a home run, two doubles and a single—but it was not enough.

In 1972 the Giants got off to their worst start in years. Now in his 21st season, Mays posed a problem for Giant owner Horace Stoneham—was Mays really worth his $125,000 salary and could Stoneham afford to pay it? Stoneham decided no, and early in the season it was announced that Willie had been traded back to New York—to the Mets.

Willie was upset, but he picked up and moved to New York. He was a sentimental hero to the Mets fans, many of whom used to root for the New York Giants. The first time the new Giants came to town, old Willie rose to the occasion, hitting a home run to beat his old teammates 5-4.

Later in the season, in his first appearance at Candlestick Park, Willie did it again, hitting another homer to beat the Giants 3-1. It was only his fourth homer of the season, but it was the 650th of his career. He hit only eight all year, and Hank Aaron passed him in career home runs.

Although older and slower, Willie was still swinging—for the New York Mets—in 1972.

As the season ended, Willie was 41. He had a career batting average of .303, was third all-time in homers with 654, fourth in extra-base hits with 1,307 and seventh in RBI's with 1,878. His slugging average was also among the top ten in history.

Late in the season he sat in the dugout before a game. Talking of his career, he said, "You add 'em up, I don't. I just play. At my age it's an accomplishment just being here."

Only time itself had been able to slow Willie down.

⚾ **Hank Aaron**

Before the 1971 All-Star game, Willie Mays and Hank Aaron were walking through the lobby of a Detroit hotel. Mays soon was surrounded by fans who wanted his autograph. Only a few asked Aaron for his signature, and some did not even seem to recognize him. Soon he was standing off to the side by the door waiting for Willie. Later, Aaron admitted, "I want Ruth's record. I guess that's the only way for me to make my mark."

By 1973 Aaron was closing in on Babe Ruth's career record of 714 home runs, and the drums were beginning to beat for him. Overshadowed by Mickey Mantle, Willie Mays and others throughout most of his baseball career, Aaron was finally moving into the spotlight.

It seemed possible that by the time he retired, "Hammerin' Hank" would establish himself as the top slugger not only of his time, but of all time. For many, his arrival at the top was a surprise. He did not approach this peak with any spectacular single-season explosions. Instead, he quietly accumulated hits and home runs with amazing consistency. He never hit 50 homers in a season, but by 1972 he had hit 20 or more in 19 straight years. At the same time, he was quietly collecting other records that would assure him a place of honor in baseball history.

Aaron had a personality all his own. He didn't do things with a flourish as did Mays. He didn't strike a pose of courage, hitting tape-measure drives on taped-up knees as did the dramatic Mantle. He didn't put off writers and fans as did the individualistic Williams. And he didn't make his private life a part of his legend as did Ruth. In some ways, he was like Jimmy Foxx, easy-going and personable. But Aaron was far more steady. He was eager to be a great hitter, but he saw his baseball achievements in perspective.

Once when he was off to a fast start, hitting .400 early in a season, someone stopped him and asked, "Aren't you Hank Aaron?"

Henry said softly, "Yes, I'm Aaron."

The other person said, "Well, don't be so modest. After all, you're hitting .400."

And Henry said, "If I was hitting .200, I'd still be Aaron."

Through most of his career, Aaron was taken for granted. He was usually recognized as one of the top hitters in the game, but not as a superstar. Magazines did not feature him as often as they did more colorful players, and no one was offering him huge amounts of money for the story of his life. Yet those that did get to know him found him to be an interesting and complicated character.

He was an intelligent man with a sly sense of

humor. He told one writer that he loved to hunt (which he does), but soon told another that he disliked hunting because the animals and the woods frightened him. Another time he reported that Stan Musial had taught him lots of little things about batting. But Musial later reported that he had never said more than "Hi" to Henry.

"Life is fun if you don't take it too seriously," Aaron once said, and writers learned that it was hard to tell when to take *him* seriously.

Pitchers in the National League learned to take Aaron seriously all the time, however. He did not swing as gracefully as a Ted Williams or a Joe DiMaggio. In fact, until he reached professional baseball, he held the bat cross-handed, with his left hand higher on the bat than his right. He hit off his front foot, and many say that he had a hitch in his swing, dropping the bat just before swinging rather than coming through with a smooth, level stroke. But appearances were deceiving.

"I've done things wrong all my life," he once said with a smile, "but I've got them done right." And his batting record proved the point.

He was so relaxed at the plate that he almost seemed to be asleep. "But he wakes up with the pitch," said Curt Simmons, a pitcher who often had to face him.

Aaron stood far back in the batter's box, and like Ted Williams, he seemed able to wait that extra split-second before swinging, seeming to hit the ball right out of the catcher's mitt. He often went after bad pitches—with good results. In one game he was walked intentionally three times. On the fourth time up, the pitcher tried to walk him again but got one of the pitches too close to the plate and Henry hit it for a home run.

In addition to his natural talents, Aaron had a student's eye for pitchers. Ted Williams once said, "Aaron knows more about the pitchers in his league than anyone else."

His season totals tell the story. Seven times he hit more than 40 home runs, and in seven other seasons he hit more than 30. He scored 100 or more runs 15 times, hit .300 or better 13 times, drove in 100 or more runs 11 times. He led the league in total bases eight times, in home runs and RBI's four times, and in batting average twice. Surprisingly, he was named Most Valuable Player only once.

"I never promoted myself," he explained. "I just went out and did the best I could and then went home. I'm no chat-chat guy."

Off the field he led a quiet life with his family. He remained close to his parents and brothers and sisters, and he spent much of his time with his own family—his wife, two sons and two daughters. And even with them he was sometimes reserved.

"I like people, but I like my privacy," he once said. "I live inside of myself a lot. I don't give a lot of myself away. I can ride a plane from L.A. to Atlanta and never make a sound or say a word. I can come home and not talk to my wife for awhile and she might think I'm mad at her. But I'm not, it's just my way, and she should know it by now."

Although he was earning more than $125,000 late in his career, he received fewer chances to make extra money off the field than other players. One reason for this was that he played in Milwaukee and Atlanta rather than in New York or Los Angeles, where players get more attention. Another reason was his race. "If a company wants a player to do a commercial and they have their choice between Tom Seaver and Henry Aaron, nine times out of ten they will take Tom," he said.

Still, he was completing his career at the very top of his profession and was steadily working his way toward baseball's most famous record—714 home runs. "It's surprising to find myself where I am," he

Aaron liked his privacy and often let his bat do the talking.

said in 1972. "I just sneaked up on everyone. I surprised even myself."

Henry Aaron was born in Down the Bay, a poor section of Mobile, Alabama, on February 5, 1934. He was the third of six children. One of his younger brothers, Tommy, also played in the major leagues for a few years and later became a player-coach in the minors.

Henry's father had moved to Mobile from the small town of Camden, where he had picked cotton for a living. In Mobile he was a boilermaker's helper at a ship-building company. When Henry was small, the family moved to Toulmanville, a better part of Mobile, and Henry's parents still live there.

When he was still in grade school, Henry was already playing baseball and softball. His father and uncles on both sides of the family had played amateur and semi-professional baseball, and they encouraged him to develop his talent. In high school he hit .700 one year. He also played football for one season and was an all-city all-star as a 150-pound guard. But he gave up the game, fearing he might get hurt and lose out on baseball. He saw his first major league teams at Hartwell Field in Mobile, where they played exhibition games on their way north from spring training. He once saw Joe DiMaggio play there.

One year the Dodgers (then in Brooklyn) held a one-day tryout camp in Mobile. Henry went out for it, but there were so many players there that he despaired of getting noticed and went home. Then a neighbor, Ed Scott, saw him playing softball and asked Henry if he would like to play pro baseball for the Mobile Black Bears. Henry asked his mother, and she said no because she was hoping he would go to college. But Henry and Scott kept asking until she finally agreed. Henry made the team and earned $5 to $10 a game, depending on how many people came to watch. He was only 15 years old. During the week he went to school and on Sundays he played for the Bears.

In 1951, when he was 17, the Indianapolis Clowns, a team in the American Black Baseball League, came to town to play the Bears. Henry, who still hit cross-handed, hit safely three times and played well at shortstop. Syd Pollock, the owner of the Clowns, was impressed.

Pollock said later, "If Henry could do that well batting cross-handed and throwing sidearm, I was curious to see what he could do if he batted right and threw right." He offered Henry $200 a month to join the Clowns. Henry's mother wanted him to go to college at Florida A&M, but Henry wanted to play pro baseball. His mother finally agreed.

In the spring of 1951 she gave him two pairs of extra pants, two dollars to put in his pocket, and two sandwiches in a brown paper bag. He was going by train to the Clowns' pre-season base at Winston-Salem, North Carolina. Henry remembered, "I was taking my first train ride and I was afraid. My mother made me take the sandwiches. She said they might not serve me on the train. They would have served me, but not for two dollars."

Although the team was called the Indianapolis Clowns, they never played there. Like the Harlem Globetrotters, they just adopted the town's name because "you had to be from somewhere." Their home was the road and they barnstormed by bus from town to town. Sometimes they slept in hotels. More often, they slept in the bus.

Henry once said, "Your roommate was the guy sitting next to you on the bus. You learned how to sleep sitting up. Otherwise you got no sleep. I learned. To this day, I can sleep anywhere any time in any position. It is the thing I do best, even better than hitting."

Sometimes the team ate in cafes for blacks only. They were not welcome in eating places for whites, but someone could order the food from the kitchen and it would be delivered to the back of the restaurant and be eaten on the bus. It was a tough way of life, but it was a way to play ball all the time.

Coaches for the Clowns made Aaron change his hitting and throwing style. By 1952 he had adjusted to the new way of doing things and began to do well. The Giants and Yankees sent scouts to watch him, and other teams began receiving reports on him. Then in a doubleheader after an all-night bus-ride, Henry hammered ten hits in eleven times up and stole two bases. Art Pollock realized that some major league team would soon take Henry. Pollock wrote to John Mullen of the Boston Braves to interest him in Aaron. Mullen sent scout Dewey Griggs to the young player with instructions to sign him. But the Giants (then in New York) also wanted him. Both teams agreed to pay the Clowns $10,000 for Henry's contract. The Giants offered a starting salary of $250 a month and the Braves offered $300 a month. That made the difference—Henry took the Braves' offer.

As Aaron later said, "Fifty dollars a month is all

that stood between me and Willie Mays being team-mates on the Giants."

Leo Durocher, then the Giant manager, had heard raves about Aaron, and when he found out the Giants had lost him for fifty dollars a month, he was furious. "It was stupid," he said years later. "So you pay a little more for a little better prospect. You take a chance. Well it cost them, for 20 years it cost them. What a team Willie and Henry would have been!"

As a bonus for signing with the Braves, Henry got a cardboard suitcase. He was assigned to Eau Claire, Wisconsin, in the Northern League to finish out the 1952 season. At 18, he broke into organized baseball, hitting .336, but making 36 errors at shortstop in 87 games. He hit only nine homers, but he showed promise of having power. He was thin at 160 pounds and inexperienced.

He was also homesick. He lived at the YMCA in the small northern town and was alone a lot. He had been exposed to prejudice, but this was his first time living as a black man in a white man's world. At one point he was talked out of returning home in a tele-phone conversation with his older brother Herb.

It was even worse for him the next season at Jack-sonville, Florida. He and two teammates were the first black players ever to play for the team. They couldn't stay in the same hotels or eat in the same restaurants as their white teammates. They had to find accomodations open to blacks elsewhere. Nei-ther the team nor the league was yet ready to go against local custom and fight for its black players' rights.

One of the first to break the color line at Jacksonville, Aaron chats with manager Ben Geraghty, who helped Hank through a tough time.

"It was depressing," Aaron admitted. Fortunately, the manager of the Jacksonville team, Ben Geraghty, helped Henry and won his admiration.

One day Henry met a girl who was taking courses at a local business college. Her name was Barbara Lucas. She had been at the game the night before and said she was sorry Henry had gone hitless. He said, "Come out again and I'll hit a few in your honor." When she did, he hit a single, a double and a homer.

He started going steady with Barbara and spent a lot of time at her house. Her father wasn't sure he wanted a baseball player as a son-in-law. Once he asked, "What other work do you do?"

Henry paused, then said, "Well, I was once in agriculture."

"Doing what?" asked the father.

"Picking strawberries," smiled Henry.

Despite the prejudices which pestered him, Henry led the league in 1953 with a .362 batting average, 125 runs batted in, 115 runs scored and 208 hits. He had switched to second base, but he led the league with 36 errors. He also led in putouts and assists and was voted Most Valuable Player. Someone wrote, "He led the league in everything except hotel accomodations."

Henry and Barbara were married on October 6th, right after the season, and he took her with him to Puerto Rico, where he played in the Puerto Rican League. The Braves told him to learn to play the outfield that winter. Mickey Owen, a former major leaguer, was his manager, and he helped Henry learn the new position.

In the spring of 1954, the Braves had moved from Boston to Milwaukee. Manager Charlie Grimm had one of the best outfields in the league—Bobby Thomson, Bill Bruton and Andy Pafko. The Braves planned to give Aaron some experience against major league pitching in spring exhibition games and then assign him to their minor league team in Toledo.

Bobby Thomson had come to the Braves from the Giants, where he had smashed his "miracle homer" to win the pennant in 1951. Aaron had gotten out of school early that day to hear the game, and he remembered being thrilled by the drama of Bobby's

blow. Now, in March of 1954, Thomson broke his
ankle sliding into second base. When Henry said he
was sorry about the accident, a veteran said, "Save
the tears, kid. This is sports. And this is your
chance."

So Aaron, who had just turned 20, tried to play
himself into Thomson's position. He doubled off the
Dodgers' star Carl Erskine in his first at-bat that
spring. Later he doubled off the Phillies' star pitcher
Curt Simmons.

Someone asked, "What did you think of him?"

"Who?" asked Aaron.

"Simmons!"

"Was that Simmons?" asked the rookie.

He tried to play it cool, but he worried, too, wondering if he would make the team. One night he tel-
ephoned his wife who was in Alabama.

"Don't make any plans yet. I still don't know
what's going to happen," he told her.

Then one night he hit a 400-foot homer which impressed everyone on the club. After the game
Grimm told him, "You're my left fielder, kid."

Barbara packed up and moved to Milwaukee.

Later Henry was shifted to right field. At first he
was assigned uniform No. 5. Later he requested a
double number because he felt it more impressive,
and was given No. 44, which he would make famous.
At first fame seemed far away, however. In his first
major league game he struck out twice, grounded
out, hit into a double play and fouled out. In one
early game he lost his cap while running the bases.
He stopped and went back to pick it up.

"When you have a choice between your cap or a

run, kid, from now on, take the run," Grimm told him.

In his second week, on April 23, Henry hit his first major league home run. He hit 13 home runs that season, but the Braves' star slugger was Eddie Mathews, a third-year third baseman who hit 40 homers. Aaron drove in 69 runs and batted .280. It was a good beginning, if not a great one.

His season was cut short on September 5 when he fractured his right ankle sliding into base. Ironically, he was replaced by Bobby Thomson, who had just recovered from his broken ankle. The Braves finished third that year, eight games behind Willie Mays' Giants. Willie had just returned from military service and was the Most Valuable Player in the league.

Milwaukee had made the Braves feel welcome. Attendance was good and the townspeople treated the players tremendously well. Before long, the Aarons bought a handsome home there, where they would raise their children. The hardest part of the trail to the top was behind Henry.

In 1955 he established himself as a regular, hitting .314 with 27 home runs, 105 runs driven home and 105 scored. He had some trouble in the field, gaining the lowest fielding average among regular outfielders, but he was developing. The team finished second, far behind Brooklyn.

When the Braves got off to a slow start in 1956, Manager Charley Grimm was removed and Fred Haney took over. The team took off and won 11 in a row to take over first place at one point. They slumped late in the season, but still finished only one game behind the Dodgers. Aaron had started slowly, too. He shrugged and said, "In a slump, all you can do is keep swinging." Then he hit in 25 straight games. He shrugged again and said, "You swing the bat, you hit the ball or you don't."

It was becoming clear to the writers and broadcasters that they could not expect colorful comments from Henry. But his .328 average was good enough to lead the league. He hit 26 homers and drove in 92 runs and was named National League Player of the Year by *The Sporting News.*

After three straight second-place finishes, the Braves were ready to come through with a pennant in 1957. They had power hitters in Eddie Mathews, Aaron and Joe Adcock and power pitching in Warren Spahn, Lew Burdette and Bob Buhl. In June they traded Bobby Thomson back to the Giants for Red Schoendienst, who solidified the infield. Then first baseman Joe Adcock broke his leg and was replaced by Frank Torre. But the Braves were not to be stopped. Aaron went wild with his bat and the Braves moved to the top of the league. More than two million baseball-mad Milwaukeeans came out to see the team, and they finished eight games ahead of second-place St. Louis.

Aaron was the key to their success. Consider one week of the season. Aaron hit a three-run homer to tie the Pirates in the ninth, then tripled and scored the winning run in the eleventh. The next night he hammered the Pirates with five straight hits. A few nights later he hit two homers and a double to beat the Bucs. Then he doomed the Dodgers with two singles, a double and a homer.

In one game, Johnny Antonelli of the Giants threatened him: "Hey, Henry, can you afford to lose some teeth?"

"Can you?" Henry replied. Then he hit Antonelli's pitch 450 feet into the upper deck. He hit three homers and drove in seven runs in the game.

He hit the 100th homer of his career August 15 in Cincinnati. Late in September he hit a homer with one on in the eleventh inning to clinch the pennant for his team. He hit his 44th and final homer of the season on the last day of the season, a grand-slam off "Sad Sam" Jones of St. Louis.

Aaron led the league in home runs, in RBI's with 132 and in total bases with 369. He batted .322 and was voted Most Valuable Player in the league. He was paid $28,500 for the season, which made him by far the lowest-paid superstar in his sport.

In the World Series the Braves beat the New York Yankees in a tense seven-game set. Lew Burdette pitched three of Milwaukee's four victories, but Aaron played a prominent part, too. He set a Series record with at least one hit in each of the seven games and led both teams with eleven hits, seven RBI's and a .393 average. He hit a home run in the third game and made a spectacular running catch of a drive by Gil McDougald with two Yankees on base. He hit a home run in the fourth game as Milwaukee won to even the Series. He tripled in the fifth game victory. He hit a tape-measure homer off the Yanks' Bob Turley in the sixth game loss. And he singled twice and scored a run as Burdette blanked the Yankees in the seventh game.

After the seventh game there was a hysterical

celebration in the Braves' dressing room. Grinning broadly, Aaron said, "This has to be the big thrill of a ballplayer's career."

Aaron's salary was raised to $40,000 for 1958, and he rewarded the Braves by helping them to a second straight pennant. He hit .326 with 30 homers as Milwaukee won again by eight games. In the World Series against the Yanks, Henry batted .333 and got nine hits. But the Braves blew a lead of three games to one. The Yankees won the last three contests and recaptured the world championship.

In 1959 Aaron got another big raise. He earned it by having the best season of his career. He led the league with a .355 batting average, a .636 slugging percentage, 223 hits and 400 total bases. He also hit 39 homers and drove in 113 runs. During the season he had one hitting streak of 22 games and he collected the 1,000th hit of his career.

The season ended with the Braves and the Los Angeles Dodgers tied for first place. But the Dodgers won two straight playoff games to take the pennant.

The disappointed Braves never recovered from the failure. Manager Haney left to take over the new Los Angeles (later California) Angels. Then a succession of managers—Charlie Dressen, Birdie Tebbetts and Bobby Bragan—tried without success to bring the Braves back to the top. Year by year, the veteran stars moved out—first Bruton, then Schoendienst, Buhl, Adcock, Burdette, Spahn, Mathews. In the next six years the Braves finished second, fourth, fifth three times, and sixth.

At the same time, the love affair between Milwaukee and the Braves faded. Attendance slipped steadily, and by 1964 there were rumors that the

Aaron and Yankee catcher Yogi Berra watch the flight of the ball as Aaron gets a hit in the 1958 World Series.

team would move south to Atlanta. They finally made the move to Atlanta before the 1966 season.

Milwaukee's black players dreaded the move to Atlanta but they found a modern and forward-looking city where the last traces of segregation were disappearing. Aaron settled his family in a fashionable brick, ranch-style house and settled himself into Braves Stadium, a shiny new park with foul lines only 330 feet long and a center-field wall only 400 feet away, all well within his reach.

During the last years in Milwaukee, as the Braves declined, Aaron continued to contribute consistently. His team didn't make national headlines and neither did he. He had no spectacular seasons, but he had one solid season after another. In Milwaukee he was his team's one shining star and became the white community's first black sports hero.

In 1960 he hit only .292, but he hit 40 home runs and led the league with 334 total bases and 126 RBI's. On July 3 he hit his 200th homer. In 1961 he hit .327 with 34 homers and 120 RBI's and led the league with 358 total bases. And in 1962 Hank hit .323 with 45 homers, 127 runs scored and 128 driven in. He also put together a second 25-game hitting streak.

Aaron's second homer of the 1963 season was the 300th of his career. At this point, Aaron's teammate, Eddie Mathews, was 100 homers ahead of him. But Hank was beginning to catch up. He led the league with 44 homers and 130 RBI's, and his .319 batting average was only seven points behind the league leader. He also stole 31 bases. He was voted Player of the Year in the National League by *The Sporting News*.

The next two seasons were disappointing for Aaron, although they would have been remarkable for most other hitters. He hit .328 in 1964 but had only 24 homers and 95 RBI's. He failed to drive in 100 runs for the first time in six years, and his home run mark was the lowest since his first year in the league. In 1965 he was sidelined with an ankle injury for the first three weeks of the season. He started slowly and finished with a .318 average, 32 homers and 89 RBI's.

In the team's first season in Atlanta in 1966, Henry batted a lowly .279, but he led the league with a .573 slugging percentage, 127 RBI's and 44 homers. His second homer of the season, on April 20, was the 400th of his career. The Braves were not

Aaron slides home safely against the Phillies, scoring a run for the new Atlanta Braves.

much improved, however, finishing fifth in the ten-team league.

Before the 1967 season Aaron signed a two-year contract for $100,000 a season. Finally, at 33, he had reached the ranks of the superstars. Mantle and Mays had reached this "magic figure" much earlier in their careers. "I suppose I should have been up in this company sooner, but I'm content to be here now," Aaron commented.

In July of 1967 he hit a homer off an old rival, Curt Simmons, then with the Cubs, and it provided Henry with the 1,500th run scored of his career. He was beginning to claim some of those large, round numbers of distinction.

"Setting records only mean you're getting old," smiled old Henry. "Ruth's record of 714 homers in a career? Man, I'm not even to 500 yet. I'll never make it."

He led the league with 39 homers that season, hit .307 and drove in 109 runs. The Braves finished a dismal seventh.

In July of 1968 Henry invited his parents to see him hit his 500th home run. His mother was sick, so his father came alone and could stay only three days. Henry tried each game to hit the homer for his father, but failed. As his father left, he said, "I'll bet you'll hit it today."

That day, Henry hit a 400-foot blast over Atlanta's left-center-field wall for his 500th. "I'm sorry my dad didn't get to see it," he said.

Willie Mays had hit his 500th homer three years earlier, but he had slowed down in the three years since, and Aaron was starting to catch up. At the end of the 1968 season Mantle retired with 536 homers and Mathews gave up with 512. Henry had hit only 29 that year, and some felt he, too, was almost through. He batted only .287, drove in only 86 runs and scored only 84. It was the first time in 14 years he had not scored 100 runs.

Late in the season, he was given a night in his honor in Atlanta, and some felt it was a sort of farewell to a player who was fading. His parents were there, along with his brothers and sisters, his wife and children. He wiped away a tear or two as he accepted his gifts before the game. Then he hit a three-run homer as if to say he wasn't finished yet.

And in 1969 he proved his point. He passed Ott's 511 and Mathews' 512 on the all-time home-run list in April. He passed Williams' 521 in June. He passed Foxx's 534 and Mantle's 536 in July. Only Mays and Ruth remained ahead of him. He hit 44 for the fourth time in his career, which was as many as he had ever hit. He hit exactly .300, drove in only 97 runs, scored an even 100, and led the league with 332 total bases.

It was a good year for the Braves, too. They won the Western Division pennant in the expanded National League. Orlando Cepeda and Rico Carty supported Aaron at the plate, and Phil Niekro led a strong pitching staff. But the season ended in disappointment when the Braves lost three straight to New York's amazing Mets in the playoff for the National League pennant. Aaron hit two doubles and three homers and drove in seven runs in the three games, but even this spectacular effort was not enough.

The Braves fell back again in 1970, but old man Aaron did not. He signed a two-year contract for

$125,000 a season and went back to work. On May 17 he hit a single in Cincinnati for his 3000th hit in the majors. Stan Musial was the only other living member of this select circle. Cincinnati fans saluted him with cheers.

Later he admitted, "Getting 3,000 hits always has been my secret goal. I never thought about Ruth's record of 714 homers. I always figured if I got the hits, the other things—the homers, the total bases, the RBI's and so forth, would fall into place. And that's about the way it's worked out."

When the 1970 season ended, he had hit 38 homers, compiled a .298 batting average and driven in 118 runs. His consistency was beginning to make a difference—it was the 14th season in which he had played in 150 or more games and the 15th in which he had scored 100 or more runs.

Fans and writers were still expecting Henry to slow down. But in 1971, at the age of 37, Hammerin' Hank had one of his greatest seasons. He batted .327 and drove in 118 runs. He hit 47 home runs—a career high—and led the league with a .669 slugging average. He hit his 600th home run on April 27 off Gaylord Perry, the outstanding San Francisco Giants' pitcher. Before the game Perry had snapped, "If he gets it off me, he's going to earn it."

After the game Aaron was told about Perry's remark. "I guess I earned it," he said with a grin.

In mid-season Aaron appeared in his 21st All-Star Game. Although he had always done well in playoffs and World Series, he had only five singles and a .181 batting average in previous All-Star competition. But in 1971 he slammed a long drive into the upper deck of the Detroit stadium against Oakland's sensational pitcher, Vida Blue.

"Maybe I'll do even better next year when we have the game in Atlanta," he suggested after the game.

In the 1972 All-Star contest he came up in the sixth inning with the National League behind. He swung, and the Atlanta crowd began to cheer when the ball left his bat and soared toward left-center. Outfielder Carl Yastrzemski jumped for it, but it went into the seats, putting the Nationals ahead. The cheering grew louder and louder. Relief pitcher Tug McGraw said, "Sitting way out in the bullpen you could feel the vibrations."

Even the players stood and applauded as Henry rounded the bases. It was an emotional moment in which Aaron was finally receiving the applause he had long deserved.

In the regular 1972 schedule, Henry hit his homers and drove in his runs, but his average slid to its lowest point ever. Finally, he confessed, "I am going for home runs now. I am swinging for them every time up. My average is suffering and I am sorry, but I can't resist any longer, I am so close to the record and time is growing so short for me I have to go for it now."

On the last day of May he hit his 648th homer to tie Willie Mays for second on the all-time home-run list. Ten days later, he hit his 649th to pass Mays. Two days after that, on June 13, Aaron came up in the tenth inning against the Mets and hit the first pitch for his 650th homer to win the game.

By mid-season 1972 two other active players had

entered the select circle of 500-homer-hitters. One, Frank Robinson, had enjoyed a remarkable career. In 1956 he tied the National League record for home runs by a rookie with 38. In 1961 he led Cincinnati's Reds to the National League pennant and was voted

As the crowd and the television cameras watch, Aaron swings for the fences.

Most Valuable Player in the circuit. Traded to Baltimore in 1966, the outfielder won the Triple Crown by leading the American League with a .316 batting average, 49 home runs and 122 runs batted in. He led the Orioles to a pennant and was voted the American League MVP, becoming the first player to win the laurel in both leagues. From 1969 through 1971 Robinson led the Orioles to three straight pennants and another World Series triumph. He hit his 500th homer late in 1971, then was traded to the Los Angeles Dodgers.

Meanwhile, Harmon Killebrew entered the 500-homer class at the age of 35 in 1971 and still was swinging toward the 600 circle in 1972. A plump, powerful, 6-foot, 210-pounder, Killebrew played for the old Washington Senators and the Minnesota Twins. He was almost exclusively a home run hitter and never batted .300 in his career. He hit more than 40 home runs in eight different seasons, however, and led the league six times. In 1965 he led the Twins to the American League pennant and was voted MVP of the league. In 1969 and 1970 he helped the Twins to divisional flags, although they lost the pennant playoffs both years.

By the end of the 1972 season, Killebrew had passed Foxx and Mantle to become the fourth greatest home run hitter behind Ruth, Aaron and Mays. It seemed unlikely, however, that Killebrew or Frank Robinson would threaten Ruth's or Aaron's home run records. Both were running out of time and they still trailed Aaron by more than 100 homers.

With no real competition left in the home run battle, Aaron continued to set other records in 1972. He became the second man in history to drive in 2,000 runs and was moving toward Ruth's record of 2,217. He became the third man in history to reach 1,300 extra-base hits and was moving toward Musial's record of 1,377. He became the second man in history to hit for 6,000 total bases and went on to break Musial's record of 6,134, finishing the season with 6,177.

Sluggers Aaron and Mays attract a crowd in 1972.

Aaron's 1972 season was solid but not spectacular. He batted .265 and drove in 77 runs. Most important, he hit 34 homers, giving him 673, only 41 short of the biggest record of all—Ruth's 714.

But he was not a statistic, nor a collection of statistics. He was not No. 44 or 714 or 715, but a man, proud, but modest, reserved but bright, and suddenly under immense pressure as he approached baseball's most famous record. A television network had already made arrangements to break into regular programming when Aaron came to bat in 1973 or 1974 to hit his 714th and 715th homers. His face was appearing on the front of magazines and newspapers, and publishers were seeking the story of his life.

"I can feel the pressure beginning to build," he said. "The closer I get, the heavier it will get, I'm sure. I'll just have to try to take it in stride. If it distracts me, I'm done. I can't begin to press, or I'll never reach my goals. I've got to stay loose."

Year after year, Aaron had surprised his fans by improving with age. But the race for the record was still a race against time. Could he hit 42 more homers before his legs and his reflexes and his eyesight broke down? "When I came into baseball I had a taste for it in my mouth and that has never changed," he said. "I still love to play. But it gets harder all the time with the travel and the night games and the long schedule. And my advancing years. Often, the fans don't realize what a player must go through and how tired he gets and what troubles he may have. But he has to go out there night after night. And the fan who goes out there once a week or once a month or once a season wants him to do his thing that night, so you got to try to give him that, you're getting paid darn well for that and he pays the bills.

"I always said I would not hang around past my prime. Not for one more paycheck or one more record. Maybe they all say that, but I don't care what anyone else says or does, I always said I wouldn't do it and I wouldn't want to do it. Not ever. I have too much pride to do that. I always wanted to go out proud.

"I still do, but it gets hard to think of quitting before you reach goals that are so close, so I hope I get to them before I begin dragging, before I feel I should get out because I can't go good any more. Maybe I've been neglected some most of my career, but I'm making up for that now and I wouldn't want to spoil it."

"If you reach 715 home runs, some will regard you as the greatest player ever," someone said.

Henry Aaron put on his most surprised expression. "Is that what that would mean?" he asked, smiling broadly.

Index

Page numbers in italics refer to photographs.